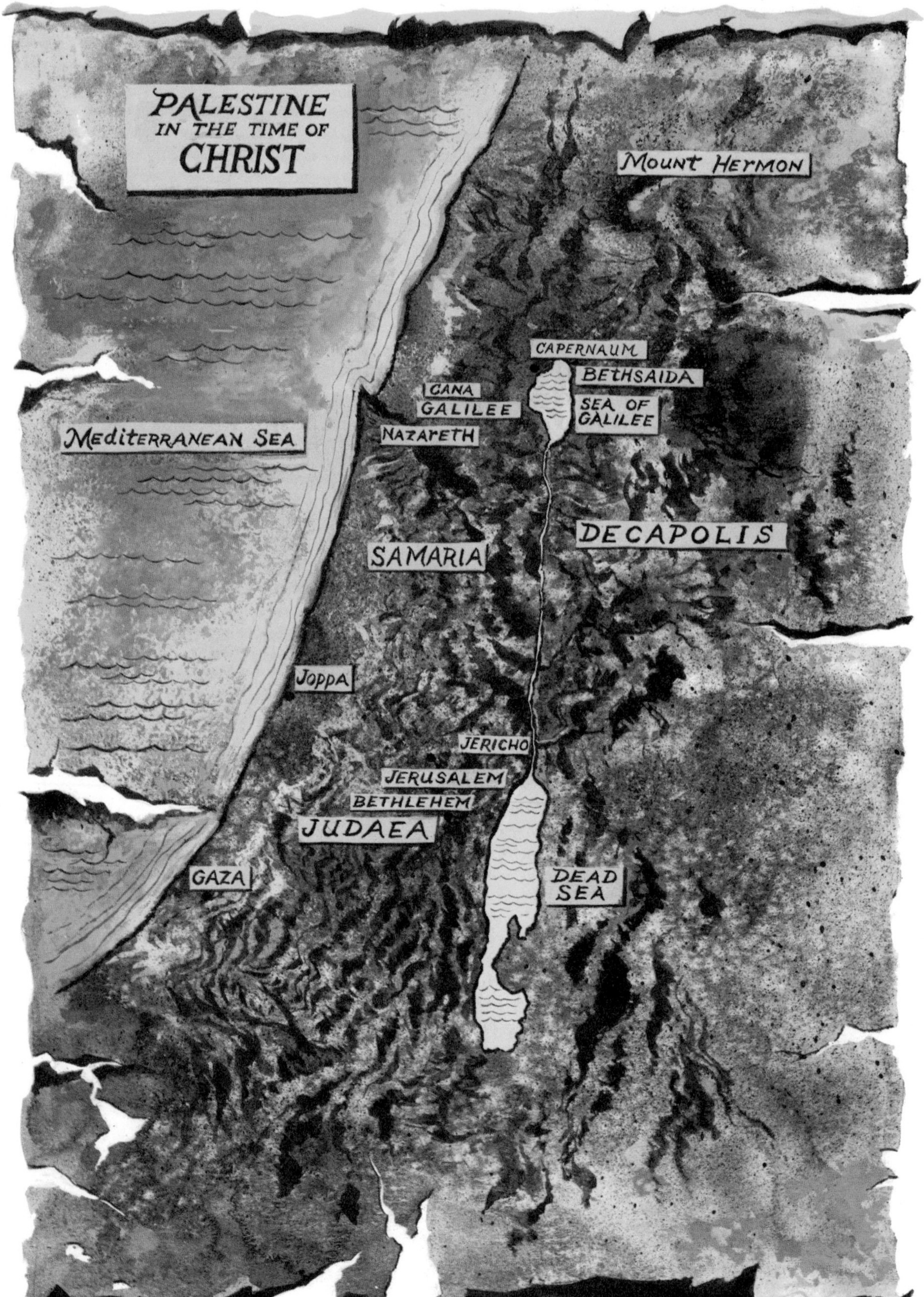

# PALESTINE
### IN THE TIME OF
# CHRIST

Mount Hermon

Mediterranean Sea

CAPERNAUM
BETHSAIDA
CANA
GALILEE
SEA OF
GALILEE
Nazareth

DECAPOLIS

SAMARIA

Joppa

JERICHO

JERUSALEM
BETHLEHEM
JUDAEA

GAZA

DEAD
SEA

# the PROMISE

by
## hal Lindsey

ILLUSTRATED BY
## norm mcGary

**HARVEST HOUSE PUBLISHERS**
Irvine, California 92707

## DEDICATION

There are two very special people whose friendship, love and prayers
have kept us inspired and encouraged
during the many long hours we've spent writing these pages.

To you, our dear friends Mike and Chris Minder, we lovingly dedicate this book
with our deepest thanks for just being there when we needed you.

*Hal and Jan Lindsey*

### SPECIAL ACKNOWLEDGMENTS

Several people deserve special thanks for their help in bringing together all the facets that
have been needed to make this a unique visual and verbal presentation of truth. Mark
Arrington, Joe Glauberg, and Fred Holtzman gave valuable help with their research.
Norman Allensworth was a great source of inspiration and encouragement to the artist
Norm McGary. My wife, Jan, once again added a special dimension to this book with her
deep insights and love for God's chosen people, the Jews.

Little did I know two years ago when I met the artist, Norm McGary, under rather unusual circumstances, that I would be collaborating on a book with him. He had sought me out after reading *The Late Great Planet Earth* to tell me that it had changed his life and had brought him out of involvement in the occult world into a new and personal relationship with the Lord.

As our friendship grew over the following months, I realized that this man was a gifted artist, having worked for years with Walt Disney and Hanna-Barbera Productions as an illustrator. As God began to take hold of his talent, he wanted to use it for Him. His first effort along that line was the cover of *There's a New World Coming*.

A few months ago he came to me with a huge portfolio of the marvelous paintings that you will see in this book. He told me that the Lord had given him a great burden to put these prophetic events from the life of Jesus into pictures but he didn't know where to go from there. Together we came up with the idea of adding several pages of narrative to each picture explaining the original Old Testament prophecy concerning these events in the life of God's Promised One, and showing their fulfillment in what happened to Jesus of Nazareth.

The pictures themselves have been a great inspiration to me as I've spent the hundreds of hours researching the material to explain them. I trust that the combined effort of Norm and I will be a challenge and inspiration to everyone who picks this book up.

**BOOKS BY HAL LINDSEY**

| | |
|---|---|
| The Late Great Planet Earth | There's a New World Coming |
| Satan is Alive and Well on Planet Earth | The Liberation of Planet Earth |
| The Guilt Trip | The Promise |

# A Promise Is a Promise

For at least four thousand years of recorded history men have looked forward with varying degrees of hope and enthusiasm to the coming of a great personage, promised by the God of Israel, who would bring peace to all mankind. Two thousand years ago, a man named Jesus of Nazareth stepped out of the Judaean hills onto a dark page of history and claimed to be that person. Thousands believed him, but many others, including the most religious men of his own nation Israel rejected him as a fraud.

For twenty decades Jesus has been the most controversial figure in the pages of literature and history. Great good and colossal evil have both been done in his name. Wars have been fought over this gentle Jewish prophet, yet his moral and ethical teachings are ranked among the most peaceable and sublime in history.

## HE DOESN'T LEAVE MEN NEUTRAL

For some impelling reason, he isn't a person that people remain neutral toward as they would with other well-known figures of history such as Abraham Lincoln or George Washington. The reasons are fairly obvious. Abraham Lincoln never dared to claim that he was the personal fulfillment of all the ancient Jewish prophecies concerning the promised Messiah. But Jesus did. He continually made the point that the things he was doing and would do were all predicted by the prophets of the Old Testament. Jesus allowed men to worship him. He often pronounced their sins forgiven. He told his followers that he and the Father in Heaven were of one and the same essence and an attempt was eventually made to stone him for blasphemy because he called himself by the ancient Jewish title of deity found in Exodus 3, "I AM".

I think you can see why it is that the more you know of the person of Jesus and his teachings, the less possible it is to remain neutral toward him or sentimentally ignorant of the real nature of what he taught.

Many people who can't swallow his claims of deity, nevertheless would like to think of him as a great philosopher and humanist, a dedicated teacher of truth. But that isn't even a credible option! If a man claims to be God and isn't, if he offers to forgive sins and can't, if his claim to be the promised Messiah is false, then this is no great teacher of truth and admirable philosopher. He's a liar and charlatan at worst or at best he's a pitiful, deluded fool.

However, there is another option open concerning this Messianic claimant. It's just possible that he was genuinely who he claimed to be, the long-awaited Messiah-King of Israel, the one whose coming was predicted for hundreds of years and eagerly awaited by oppressed men through centuries of suffering and persecution.

The basic premise of this book is that it's not only *possible* that Jesus was Messiah, but that the only fair-minded conclusion that can possibly come from an honest and open investigation of the historical and Biblical evidence is that he is *indeed* Messiah.

I'm fully aware that just to make that statement means that many people will read no further in this book. But that's the privilege and the risk that comes with having the kind of freedom of mind and soul that God has given men. I can't and wouldn't force another to come to the same conclusions that I have about who Jesus is. But my intellectual integrity compels me to offer as critically as I can in the following words and pictures, the record of historical evidence and the weight of fulfilled prophecy to show why no other figure in all of human history has ever, or could ever quality to be the promised Messiah of God, except Jesus of Nazareth.

## THE GROUNDS OF MESSIANIC CONVICTION

There have been hundreds of men and women in history whose religious and political philosophies have stirred the souls of countless enraptured followers. Most of their movements have died, taking the name of their founder with them. Others have lived on and gained large and dedicated followings.

With millions of people convinced of Judaism, Mohammedanism, Buddhism, and Communism (just to name a few of the more popular movements of our day), how is it that followers of Jesus still insist that he *alone* is worthy to be followed and is the only sure way to know the one true God of this universe? This is either unbelievable bigotry or it is genuine conviction based upon grounds that appear to be so irrefutable that they leave no other possible conclusion.

What are those grounds that have undergirded the faith of millions of people in Jesus?

They are the same grounds that led Jesus himself to claim that he was the Messiah and therefore the *only* path to God the Father. The credentials of his Messiahship which he presented to his followers was the evidence of fulfilled prophecy in his life.

## MESSIAH'S PROPHETIC CREDENTIALS

Prophecy itself is not unique to the Bible. Hundreds of psychics and religious seers have made predictions of the future during their lifetimes and some have had a degree of accuracy. But what is unique to the Bible is that it has been 100 percent accurate in *every* prophecy fulfilled to date.

I realize that's an enormous statement to make and unfortunately the limited space here won't permit me to take these hundreds of Biblical prophecies and demonstrate their accurate fulfillment. I have selected, however, about 36 of the more than 300 predictions in the Old Testament which relate to its most important prophetic theme, the promise of a Messiah-deliverer who would be sent by God to create the Kingdom of God on earth, restore the Jews to their land and bring all men and nations into an earthly and eternal peace.

This Promised One of God was spoken of by at least twenty of the Old Testament writers living at different times in history and in greatly varying circumstances. The differing names they called him all spoke of

his message and ministry. Moses called him *Shiloh*, the rightful ruler (Genesis 49:10). At another time he spoke of him as *The Prophet like Moses himself* (Deuteronomy 18:15-19). In 1 Chronicles 17:11-15 he's called *The Son of David*. Years later Isaiah adds that this 'Son' will sit on the throne of David his father and be known as the *Eternal King of David's Throne* (Isaiah 9:6). Jeremiah referred to him as the *Righteous Branch of David* and *Jehovah our Righteousness* (Jeremiah 23:5, 6). King David in Psalm 2:2 called him *Jehovah's Anointed One.* One of the most often referred to titles of Messiah was Isaiah's portrait of him as the *Servant of the Lord* (Isaiah 53:11).

There were many other names for God's Anointed Servant who was to come, and stroke by stroke a portrait emerged through the early centuries of Judaism's history of this great anticipated Deliverer. Minute details of his ancestry, forerunner, birthdate, birthplace, infancy, manhood, teaching, character, career, preaching, reception, rejection, death, burial, resurrection and ascension were all prewritten in the Jewish prophets.

However, through these prophecies it became clear that this Messiah would not only appear for the blessing of the nation of Israel, but as Isaiah the prophet wrote, he would bring forth justice to the whole world and be the light and salvation of the Gentile nations also (Isaiah 42:1; 49:5, 6).

## THE PROMISED 'SEED'

The first mention of the appearance of this Promised One is found right after the first mention of sin in the Bible. In Genesis 3:15 God told Adam and Eve that there would be a future *seed* of a woman who would bruise the head of Satan. Christian and Jewish commentators alike saw this as a prediction of this coming Deliverer and his role in undoing the damage which Satan had done to mankind's relationship with God.[1]

Nothing more was written about this Promised *Seed* until around the year 2000

---

[1]Explicitly referred to as messianic in Targum Jonathan and Jerusalem Targum (2nd and 3rd century C. E. Jewish writings).

B.C.E.[1] when God called a man named Abram (Abraham) to leave his home in Ur of the Chaldees and go to a far off land which God promised to give him. God made an agreement *(covenant)* with Abraham that if he would go to this unknown land that He had chosen for him, great blessings would come to him personally and to his descendants. Their numbers would be as vast as the sands of the sea and through this *seed* of Abraham the whole world would eventually be blessed (Genesis 12:1-3).

The word *seed* is a collective noun and no doubt refers primarily here collectively to all of the future children of Abraham. But ancient Jewish and Christian writers also saw this as a further reference to the Promised *Seed* of Genesis 3:15 who came to be known among the descendants of Abraham as the 'Anointed One' or *ha-mashi'ah* from which we get our anglicized word *Messiah*.[2]

### THE ABRAHAMIC COVENANT

There were other facets to this Abrahamic Covenant. Besides making Abraham's name great and blessing him personally, God also vowed that He would bless those people who blessed Abraham and curse those who cursed him. Ancient and modern history give evidence to the fulfillment of this prediction as you trace the fate of nations who persecuted the Jews and those who supported them.

There were other extremely important promises embodied in the Abrahamic Covenant. Abraham was to become the father of many nations, not just one. Kings would come from his lineage and God would be the God of Abraham and his seed forever, for God's covenant with His chosen people was to be an everlasting covenant (Genesis 17:1-8).

The promise of a specific piece of real-estate that came to be known as the Promised Land is perhaps the most controversial part of God's covenant with Abraham. But in Genesis 15:18-20 the entire area from the River of Egypt (not the Nile, but an ancient one thought to be in the area of the present Suez Canal) to the Euphrates River was given to Abraham and his posterity as an eternal possession *forever*.

Eventually Abraham had many sons, but the promises of the Covenant were renewed to only one of his sons, Isaac, for we read in Genesis 21:12, "… in Isaac shall your seed be called." Isaac had twin sons, Jacob and Esau, but for reasons known only to a sovereign God, Jacob was the one chosen through whom God's promises of the covenantial relationship with Abraham's seed was to continue (Genesis 28:13, 14).

### WHY ARE ABRAHAM'S DESCENDANTS THE 'CHOSEN PEOPLE'?

There have been myriads of people throughout history who have greatly resented the concept of a 'chosen people'. They've wondered why God found it necessary to isolate one nation and give it such providential treatment. Did it mean that the Jews (the name given to Abraham, Isaac and Jacob's physical descendants) were better than other people? (Deut. 9:1-6).

It might be good to look briefly at the world of Abraham's day and then see more readily why God chose a specific group of people to bear His name and reputation among the billions of people who would live on this earth.

The spiritual condition of mankind was at a low ebb in God's estimation when He gave His call to Abraham. A great deal of time had elapsed since God had first created man and revealed to him the joys and responsibilities of having a relationship with a holy and personally knowable God. Since that rebellious day when he first sinned, man had drifted so far from God that about 500 years before Abraham, God had judged the world for its unholy and idolatrous ways by destroying most of mankind with a great flood.

Although this awful judgment brought men back to the worship of the one true God for awhile, they gradually began to drift into polytheism again and by the time of Abraham's day, the whole world was

---

[1] B.C.E.—*Before the Common Era*, or the time of Christ—C.E.—*Common Era* is used to designate the age since Christ.

[2] Soncino Edition of the Pentateuch and Haftorahs, edited by Dr. J. H. Hertz, Late Rabbi of the British Empire, Soncino Press.

pretty far gone into paganism.

It's amazing that God could find one man like Abraham who was still sensitive enough to hear the voice of God and then so faithfully act upon what he was told to do. But God had a plan for drawing mankind back to Himself and He needed just such a man and his descendants to be His 'showcase' to the world. There were no doubt many ways in which God planned to use His chosen people, not only by what He did *through* them, but also by what he often had to do *to* them. I've listed what I feel are four of the most important reasons for God calling the Hebrew race into existence.

## FOUR MISSIONS FOR THE JEWS

The *first reason* was that their prophets were to receive and write down God's revelation of Himself and His will for mankind. They were also to record the history of His dealings with their race and with the other nations whose destinies crossed theirs. They not only faithfully did this but they also wrote down things, under the inspiration of God's Spirit, which were future (prophetic) in nature and of which they could have had no personal understanding of its meaning at that time (I Pet. 1:10-12).

The *second reason* the Jews were chosen was to protect and preserve for posterity the textual purity of the Scriptures God inspired them to write. The degree of success which the Jewish scribes and Rabbis had in doing this is one of the wonders of the ancient times. For centuries holy men of Israel gave their whole lives to copying, studying and interpreting their Law as given to Moses and also the writings of the prophets.

The *third reason* the Jewish nation was called into existence was so that they could be a witness to a darkened pagan world that there was only one true God, a God of light and life who loved mankind and wanted it to be reconciled to Him. By their love and devotion to God and by His providential care for them, the Jews were to be a light to the Gentile nations to show them how to come to know God and His truth. Throughout their four thousand years of existence, the Jews were not always willing witnesses of this to the world. However,

even their rebellion and subsequent discipline of twice being taken into dispersion all over the known world spread the word of Jehovah God to the heathen nations who might never have heard of Him any other way.

The *fourth reason* for Israel's continued miraculous existence and the one that's most relevant to this book, is that this was to be the ethnic people through which the Messiah, the Savior of the world would be born. More than once Satan tried to completely annihilate this race of people, primarily so that he could prevent their Messiah from being born. During the reign of Queen Esther, the Jewish maiden who was married to the Persian King Ahasuerus, a monstrous anti-Semitic plot was hatched by the king's right-hand counselor, Haman, which was designed to kill all the Jews. Fortunately God used the King's love for Esther to turn this situation from its evil course and the Jews were saved.

## DAVID'S LINE PRESERVED

On another occasion, during the years when King David's descendants were reigning over the Nation of Judah, there was a wicked king named Ahaziah who led the people away from God. His main advisor was his evil mother, Athaliah. When her son died, she usurped the throne and had all the royal seed of the House of David killed, or so she thought. Unknown to her, God had seen to it that one of the year-old sons of the king, a child named Joash was hidden with his nurse in the House of the Lord until he was seven years old. Then he was brought forth and proclaimed King and his wicked grandmother, who had been falsely ruling as Queen, was put to death (2 Chronicles 22:1-12; 23:1-15).

Here's the point of this story, however. Had *all* the legal heirs to David's throne been destroyed, there could never have been a 'Greater Son of David' born at a later time in history to reign from his father David's throne *forever* as Nathan the prophet had predicted (1 Chronicles 17:11-15). The lineage of King David through his son Solomon, which had the legal inheritance to the throne, would have ceased to exist right then. But God, in His plan to bring Messiah to this world, was not to be thwarted by the schemes of men. He had said that a Son of David would reign forever over the kingdom of God and nothing was going to stop that from happening.

## THE PARADOX OF ANTICIPATION AND REJECTION OF MESSIAH

What you've read so far has been presented to you through the eyes and mind of a non-Jew, a Gentile, who has studied the Old Testament regularly for over fifteen years and usually in the officially accepted Hebrew Massoretic text. I've also studied the Greek New Testament with equal fervor and profit. As a result of all of this study, it seems overwhelmingly obvious to me that the Messiah, which the Jews so passionately longed for, came to this world 2000 years ago in the person of Jesus of Nazareth.

Yet, the question that continues to plague me and so many other serious students of the Bible is, "Why wasn't it that obvious to the Jews of that day that this was their Messiah? He continually pointed to the things he did and said and declared that these were fulfillments of their own prophetic scriptures? Couldn't they have checked this out and seen the truth or error of it?

There's no simple answer to that question! Many thousands of Jews did proclaim him as their Messiah and became new men and women as they followed him and his teachings, but why didn't the majority of religious leaders, who knew the prophecies concerning Messiah, give Jesus their support and proclaim him to the people as the Promised One of God?

## THE JEWISH MIND OF JESUS' DAY

In order to answer these questions, we need to look at what was going on in Judaism in the centuries preceding Christ. We have to be aware of the fact that the Old Testament doesn't record it all for us. The Judaism which many Bible students think existed during Jesus' day and the Judaism which really held sway over the masses are two quite different things.

One word sums up what has really held sway over all Judaism since their last prophet Malachi spoke to them about 400 years before Christ and that word is TRA-DITION! Tradition about God, tradition about His Laws (Torah), tradition about how to live, eat, work, worship, marry and even die.

Now there's nothing basically wrong with tradition and if the Jews hadn't had it, God would have had a lot harder time preserving them intact as a continuous nation for 4000 years. No matter which nation they found themselves in bondage to at any given time in history, it didn't upset the flow of their daily lives and worship of their God because that was all set out for them by tradition. As the walls of their various ghettos squeezed in on them, their whole lives revolved around their Rabbis, their synagogues, their Laws, their love for and longing to see the Holy City, Jerusalem, and their expectation of Messiah coming to deliver them and return them to Eretz Israel.

Unfortunately, because their Laws and traditions required that they live quite differently from the people in whose midst they often found themselves, this 'strangeness' on the part of the Jews caused them to be the butt of great ridicule, suspicion and hostility. This, plus the accusation they received of being the ones who crucified Christ, was the source of mob rampages through Jewish settlements and towns which through their history accounted for the death of millions of innocent Jews.

## THE DEVELOPMENT OF TRADITION

When did all these traditions become such an integral part of Judaism and how did they begin to take the place of the *actual words* of Moses and the Prophets themselves in the daily lives of the followers of Jehovah God?

Hundreds of volumes have been written to answer those questions so all I can do here is give the briefest summary.

For 70 years in the 6th century B.C.E. the Jews found themselves as captives in Babylon and their beloved city of Jerusalem and Solomon's glorious temple lay in devastation and neglected ruin. When Babylon was defeated by the Media-Persian Empire in 539 B.C.E. a new day began for the captive Jews. The Persian King Cyrus liked the Jews and gave them permission to return to their land as free men or stay in Babylon if they chose. Though the mass of the nation chose to remain, the captivity was officially at an end.

The return of the Jews to their land was accomplished in three separate expeditions. The first company returned under the leadership of Zerubbabel, a prince of Judah, and consisted of less than fifty thousand Jews. Within twenty years they had rebuilt their temple and reinstated temple worship.

About 78 years later, the second expedition of a small zealously religious group of pilgrims led by Ezra returned to Jerusalem. Upon his arrival he found gross immoralities and unsound religious practices and abuses everywhere. From this, these religious leaders could see that the people had to have a rigid code of laws to live by or Judaism would not long survive. Ezra led the task of assembling and arranging all of the Mosaic Law and writings of the Jewish prophets into basically what we now know as the Old Testament.

Meanwhile the third expedition of Babylonian Jews back to Jerusalem took place under Nehemiah's leadership in 444 B.C.E. When he saw the desolation of the city and the broken down walls, he gathered the people together, and despite the bitter opposition from some of the half-Jews (Samaritans) and non-Jews who lived in the area, in 52 days the walls of Jerusalem were rebuilt and the city became prosperous once again with the people revived in their worship and service to God.

## NO MORE PROPHETS IN THE LAND

In the meantime, when the last recognized Jewish prophet, Malachi, preached and wrote his final words in about the year 400 B.C.E., the people were left without a direct voice from God. In the absence of fresh revelation from God. devout men of Judaism began to give themselves totally to the study and minute interpretations of the Law. From morning till night, day after day and year after year they dissected the Law in an effort to be sure that there was no way in which the people might be breaching its intent in their daily conduct in any way, shape or form.

Generation by generation a mass of oral and written laws dealing with religious, moral and civil issues accumulated alongside the actual scriptures themselves and in fact, for most Jews, was a greater authority in their lives than the actual scriptures were. The interpretation and application to the people of these laws, as well as the Scriptures, was left primarily in the hands of the religious leaders. The Sages, Teachers, Scholars, Rabbis, scribes or whatever else they were called at any given time in Jewish history were the ultimate authorities on what God had to say to man.

## THE MESSIANIC PARADOX

Perhaps nowhere were the people more dependent on the knowledge of the Rabbi than in the matter of what the Messiah would be like. And yet, this very subject was the source of widest variance of views among the scholars themselves. This is because of the obvious contradictions of the character and role of the Messiah which emerged out of prophetic passages of scripture which most of the Jewish expositors accepted as truly Messianic.

These seeming contradictions centered around a two-fold picture of Messiah: One who would come as a conquering King, restoring the Jews to their land and reigning in peace over the whole world, and the other a Messianic figure who appeared to be humble and suffering, bearing the sins of the people and making atonement for them before God. Sometimes in the same prophetic passage of scripture this contrast was seen, such as in Isaiah 52:13 and 14 where it speaks of the Servant of the Lord (referring to Messiah) as prospering and being high and lifted up and greatly exalted. Then it also speaks of him as being one whose appearance is marred more than that of any man. In other words, he would experience both exaltation and humiliation.

Another point of seeming contradiction was whether Messiah would be a human being of extraordinary powers and abilities or whether he would in fact be God Himself. A number of the Messianic prophecies spoke of him as being both. An example of this is Isaiah 9:6 where it says that the Messiah would be born as a child, thus making him a human being and yet in the same verse he's called The Mighty God, The Everlasting Father and the Prince of Peace, all names that are indicative of God alone, thus implying that Messiah would somehow be both man and God.[1]

There was no common agreement on this particular issue among the Jewish expositors. For example Rabbi Akiva (2nd Century C.E.) was convinced that the Jewish rebel leader Bar Kokhba was the Messiah and yet he also taught that Messiah would occupy a throne alongside God. There are references in both the Talmud and Midrash to the immortality of Messiah and yet Rabbi Hillel (4th Century C.E.) denied that Messiah was coming at all.[2]

## THE MESSIAH THE JEWS WANTED, AND THE ONE THEY GOT!

On a strictly pragmatic level, what the Jews of Jesus' day really wanted in a Messiah was someone who would fulfill all of the predictions of a great deliverer and King; someone who would drive out the hated Roman rulers from the land and take the Jewish throne away from the Idumean usurper, Herod. All they had known for centuries was suffering and persecution and their longing for deliverance from all of that was very acute.

Because of this, there were those who appeared from time to time claiming to be the Messiah. They usually came with dreams of political overthrow and in the end, it was they who were overthrown and most of their names have been lost to history.

But that was not the case in the year 29 C.E.. Eight centuries before, the Prophet Amos had predicted that there would be a time in Israel when there would be such a famine and thirst for the Word of God that the people would stagger to and fro seeking to hear the Word (Amos 8:11). That was truly the case with the mass of Judaism in Jesus' day. The religious leaders had made such a hedge around the Word thinking to protect it, and in so doing, made it so that no

one could get near the true Word. Isaiah predicted that this would happen. He said the time would come when the people would draw near to God with their words and honor Him with their lips, but their hearts would be far from Him and their reverence would consist of tradition learned by rote (Isaiah 29:13).

These were the very words that Jesus threw back at the Pharisees and scribes who were criticizing his disciples for eating with unwashed hands which was against one of their traditions. When they accusingly said to him, "Why don't your disciples walk according to the tradition of the elders?," Jesus said to them, "Rightly did Isaiah prophesy of you hypocrites, as it is written, 'THIS PEOPLE HONORS ME WITH THEIR LIPS, BUT THEIR HEART IS FAR AWAY FROM ME. BUT IN VAIN DO THEY WORSHIP ME, TEACHING AS DOCTRINES THE PRECEPTS OF MEN.' Neglecting the commandment of God, you hold to the tradition of men" (Luke 7:5-8).

## THE REFRESHING APPEAL OF JESUS

There were many things that made Jesus unique and appealing to the masses of his day. His miracles were like nothing the people had ever seen before. His philosophy that they should do good to their enemies was new to their ears. His whole approach to the idea of worshipping and serving God was different than anything they'd been taught. Whereas the teachings of Judaism were concerned mainly with a man's external and outward behavior, it left the inner man, the spring of actions, untouched. Jews knew that they committed what God would call 'sins,' but they didn't feel that these sprang from any inborn nature of sin but was something which could be disciplined out of a man by study of the Law, prayer and good works.

It was in this area where there was the most fundamental difference between Jesus' teachings and Rabbinism. Judaism started with the demand of outward obedience and righteousness and pointed to Sonship as its goal. Jesus said that man's biggest problem was the inner problem of a nature that was sinful and he offered a free gift of forgiveness to men for their sins thereby making them Sons of God. Then he de-

[1]Targum Jonathan Ben Uzziel

[2]Encyclopaedia Judaica, *Messiah*, page 1411.

clared that obedience and righteousness would be the inevitable result of Sonship. He offered to give men a new heart, new hope for eternal life, a cleansing and forgiveness of their sins and a new Father-son relationship with God with all the privileges bound up in that.

When he taught, as in the Sermon on the Mount, he would say, "You've heard it taught that the ancients were told," and then he would go on and quote one of the external commandments which had been handed down in their traditions. Then he astounded the people by saying to them, "But *I* say to you it isn't just sinful *actions* that will be judged by God, but the *motives* in a man's heart that made him do the action, as well."

The people could see from this that he didn't speak as the Scribes and Pharisees who were forever quoting other scholars in support of their teachings. He spoke as one having the authority of God within himself. He told the Jewish leaders, "You search the Scriptures, because you think that in them you have eternal life, and it is these that bear witness of Me: and you are unwilling to come to Me, that you may have life" (John 5:39, 40).

In one sentence, Jesus put his finger on the problem with men of that day and with unbelievers of all time. He said that he was the way, the truth and the life but that men must be willing to come to him if they would have eternal life (John 14:6). Through the pictures and pages that follow, my earnest desire is that you will see for yourself that he is who he claimed to be, God's Messiah, the Savior of mankind, and that you will be drawn to him for eternal life.

**GENESIS 3:15**

And I will put enmity between you and the woman, and between your seed and her seed; He shall bruise you on the head, and you shall bruise him on the heel.

ואיבה אשית בינך ובין האשה
ובין זרעך ובין זרעה הוא ישופך
ראש ואתה תשופנו עקב :

The Seed of Woman

# The Seed of Woman

The story of Adam and Eve in the beautiful Garden of Eden is perhaps the oldest story ever recorded in human history. There are those who can't accept it as more than just a myth to explain the origin of man, but others see it as a literal happening and the beginning of man's existence and his troubles on this earth.

Whichever view you hold, it's not a very happy story. For in this narrative, man, who begins with such supreme potential and unlimited fellowship with his Creator God, succumbs to the temptings of an evil spirit-being known as Satan and as a result begins to experience the heartache of judgment and alienation from God.

## EVIL REARS ITS UGLY HEAD

With this introduction of evil into the human race, the consequences of rebellion, guilt, self-will, selfishness and death begin to manifest themselves, first in Adam and Eve and then in their children, beginning with Cain killing his brother Abel.

That there is evil in the world is evident to honest men everywhere. You can't read the morning paper without seeing it in glaring black and white. It's also true that the world is simply the sum total of all the individuals in it, each with his own attitudes of self-centeredness, intolerance and rebellion. Thus, the distresses which ail this world are simply an amplification of those which ail each of us as individuals.

The wayward tendency in mankind is so self-evident that some explanation for its origin must be found. If we're to believe the consistent Biblical record, then we must accept the fact that Satan's subtle temptings of Adam and Eve, enticing them to disregard God's expressed will, led them into an act and attitude of rebellion against God which is the heart of what the Bible thereafter describes as *sin*.

Theologians argue about whether man's disposition to sin is something which was introduced as a taint in all flesh from Adam's day on, or whether man simply gets around to sinning because he catches it like a disease from those around him. This isn't a mute question, because sin is far too prevalent in the world for us to say that it's found in greater degrees in some societies and cultures than in others. If all men were born good or even morally neutral, you'd expect to find some places in this world where sin, by any reasonable standard of measurement, has no great foothold. But that isn't the case.

The Bible, Old and New Testaments, makes no bones about the fact that men are *not* born morally neutral. They're born with a predilection to rebel against God and it will eventually bring them to a place of expression of that rebellion in some act of *failing* to do God's will or doing something *against* His will, both of which are considered sin by all the writers of the Bible.

## GOD HAS THE LAST WORD

When Satan did his dirty work in the Garden, he was really seeking to divert the worship of this new creature, man, away from God and to himself. The lie he used on Adam and Eve about why God didn't want them to eat of a certain tree, was that God knew the fruit of that tree would make men as wise as God Himself and God didn't want to share His glory with any of His creatures.

To their great sadness, Adam and Eve found that, far from making them as wise as God, the deceptive fruit lost them their sense of fellowship and communication with Him. They no longer had uninhibited access into their loving Creator's presence. In fact, a barrier was erected between them and God—a barrier so real that no one but God Himself could remove it and reestablish a relationship with man.

This is where the promise of Genesis 3:15 came in. In this conversation which God had with Satan after man's fall, God put a curse on him and pronounced that a time would come when a future descendant of Eve, called the 'seed of the woman' would destroy Satan and his work like a man grinding a snake's head under his foot. This 'seed of the woman' would give Satan a fatal blow but in return it was said that Satan would damage him, as if he were bruised on the *heel*. That is, a painful blow but not a fatal one as a blow on the head would be.

This is an intriguing prophecy. The phrase 'seed of the woman' is an unusual description. Normally people spoke of the seed of the man or the father, but rarely, if ever, of the seed of the woman. In the ancient Near East where the Bible was written, descendants were always regarded as the sons or daughters of the father. For instance, all the genealogies of the Bible are traced through the fathers, not the mothers.

The ancient rabbis realized that this passage spoke of the Messiah, for in the Targums, the ancient translations of the Old Testament into Aramaic, this passage was paraphrased to refer to the Messiah.* In some way, which I'm sure they couldn't comprehend then, God's Promised One, the Messiah, was to be the offspring of a woman in some unique way.

## THE LINEAGE OF THE PROMISED 'SEED'

Once God had made this commitment to send someone into the world to destroy Satan and thus undo his work in the lives of men, a highway was prepared in future history for the steps of this Promised One. It first began with God singling out one man, Abraham, and his descendants, and making a covenant with him that "in his seed" all the nations of the earth would eventually be blessed (Genesis 12:1-3). So the first prerequisite of the coming deliverer was that he would have to be a descendant of Abraham

Abraham had no children at the time that God made this promise to give him sons "like the sands of the sea." Yet, after a time

---

*Targum Pseudo-Jonathan and the so-called Jerusalem Targum

of unbelief during which Abraham fathered a child named Ishmael, who was *not* the intended heir to this promise, Abraham and Sarah eventually gave birth to Isaac, the son which God intended to be in the lineage of his Promised Seed.

Isaac had twin sons, Jacob and Esau, but for reasons known only to God, Jacob was the one chosen through whom God's Covenantial promises would continue. Jacob had twelve sons who became the founders of the twelve tribes of the Nation of Israel. As Jacob was about to die, he predicted the tribe through which the promised 'seed', who would uniquely bless all nations, would come. He called his sons together and forecast, "The sceptor shall not depart from [*his son*] *Judah,* nor the ruler's staff from between his feet, until SHILOH comes, and to him shall be the obedience of the peoples" (Genesis 49:10).

This prophecy not only declared the tribe through which the Messiah would come, but it designated Judah as the royal line for future kings. Rabbinic interpretation from ancient times recognized 'Shiloh' as a personal title of Messiah and that it was here predicted that he would come from the tribe of Judah.

The Jerusalem Targum paraphrases this prophecy this way, "There shall not cease kings from the house of Judah, nor scribes teaching the law from his children's children until the time that [*shiloh*] King Messiah shall come, whose is the kingdom, and to him are all the kingdoms of the earth to be subjected. How fair is King Messiah, who is hereafter to arise from the house of Judah...."

## IS 'SHILOH' SOON TO COME?

It's no coincidence to me that on the very day in which I've written these words my eyes fell on an article in the newspaper, the Jerusalem Post, September 24, 1974, issue. The article was speaking about the Jewish New Year, Rosh Hashana. "Students of the Kabbala (*Jewish mystics*) noted that the Hebrew equivalent of the New Year 5735, ending in the word "Shilo," is the name of the Messiah, and that it predicts his coming *this year.*"

Even so, come quickly, Lord Messiah!

# Prophecy of David's Greater Son

**1 CHRONICLES 17:11-15**

"And it shall come about when your days are fulfilled that you must go to be with your fathers, that I will set up one of your descendants after you, who shall be of your sons; and I will establish his kingdom. He shall build for Me a house, and I will establish his throne forever. I will be his father, and he shall be My son; and I will not take My lovingkindness away from him, as I took it from him who was before you. But I will settle him in My house and in My kingdom forever, and his throne shall be established forever." According to all these words and according to all this vision, so Nathan spoke to David.

והיה כי מלאו ימיך ללכת עם-אבתיך
והקימותי את-זרעך אחריך אשר יהיה
מבניך והכינותי את-מלכותו : הוא
יבנה-לי בית וכננתי את-כסאו עד-
עולם : אני אהיה-לו לאב והוא יהיה-
לי לבן וחסדי לא-אסיר מעמו כאשר
הסירותי מאשר היה לפניך : והעמד-
תיהו בביתי ובמלכותי עד-העולם
וכסאו יהיה נכון עד-עולם : ככל
הדברים האלה וככל החזון הזה כן
דבר נתן אל-דויד :

**MATTHEW 22:41-42**

Now while the Pharisees were gathered together, Jesus asked them a question, saying, "What do you think about the Christ, whose son is He?" They said to Him, "The son of David."

# Prophecy of David's Greater Son

As God stood in the Garden of Eden with fallen man at His side, and gave him the promise that one day a seed of the woman would come and bring about a reconciliation with man, He was looking down the corridors of time ahead at the line of descent that would be necessary to bring this one into the world. First He designated the nation this Promised One would come from, Israel. Then his lineage was narrowed to the tribe of Judah, one of the twelve sons of Jacob.

Finally at around 1000 B.C.E. the last prediction limited the line of the Messiah to one family within the tribe of Judah, the family of David. David was one of the greatest men in Israel's history. He had risen from tending sheep in the obscure town of Bethlehem to replace the Jews' first king, Saul. David was a military genius, prophet, poet and king. One of his most important contributions to the nation was his capturing of the Jebusite city of Jerusalem and making it the religious and secular center of Judaism.

One day it occurred to David that while he had a lovely house of cedar to dwell in, the most important religious article in the possession of the Jews, the ark of the Covenant of the Lord, did not have a permanent place to reside but was moved from tent to tent. When David told the prophet Nathan of this concern, the Lord gave a message to Nathan to give to David. The heart of the message was this, "I took you from the shepherd's field and made you a ruler over My people Israel and I have been with you everywhere you've gone and have dealt with your enemies and made your name great. Now, I appreciate your desire to build a house for Me, but I, the Lord, plan to build a house for *you*" (1 Chronicles 17:1-10, paraphrase).

## THE ETERNAL 'HOUSE' OF DAVID

The two houses being spoken about here were two different things. God was speaking of an eternal house, an everlasting dynasty that He was going to bring about through David's descendants. David had in mind a physical building in which the ark could be placed and the Lord worshipped. David hoped to build a magnificent edifice for the Lord, but in the end he was forbidden to do so because God said he had been a man of war.

But the house the Lord had in mind for David was going to be one which *He*, God, would build and it would be both His and David's house. These are the words of the prophet Nathan as he stood before the king and gave him the Lord's message, "And it shall come about when your days are fulfilled that you must go to be with your fathers, that I will set up one of your descendants after you, who shall be of your sons; and I will establish his kingdom. He shall build for Me a house, and I will establish his throne forever. I will be his father, and he shall be My son; and I will not take My lovingkindness away from him, as I took it from him who was before you. But I will settle him in My house and in My kingdom forever, and his throne shall be established forever" (1 Chronicles 17:11-14).

## THE DAVIDIC COVENANT

David was guaranteed at least three unique things in this prophetic promise. First, he was assured that one of his own blood descendants would be established on his throne by God Himself. In those days when governments were fairly precarious, it must have given great comfort to David to know for sure that his lineage would continue on Israel's throne.

Secondly, this descendant from among his sons would be absolutely unique because he would rule upon David's throne *forever*.

Thirdly, this exalted son of David would have a unique relationship with God as Father-Son. The passage in Hebrew literally says, "I, Myself, will be to him for a Father, and he will be to Me for a Son" (verse 13). The Hebrew construction here indicates a very strong and unique Father-Son relationship between this son of David and God that has no parallel anywhere else in the Old Testament.

## SOLOMON WAS DAVID'S SON, BUT NOT HIS 'GREATER SON'

Some interpreters of recent times have sought to teach that this prophecy was fulfilled by Solomon and was intended to refer only to him. There are many reasons why this has no validity. I'll mention just two.

First, many prophets who lived *after* David and Solomon spoke of a *future* fulfillment of this prediction. In about 750 B.C.E., some 200 years *after* Solomon's time, Isaiah spoke of the Messiah ruling from David's throne at a time in the future (Isaiah 9:6, 7).

Ezekiel, in about 650 B.C.E., also spoke of this predicted son of David, "Behold, the days are coming, declares the Lord, when I shall raise up for David a righteous Branch; and He will reign as king and act wisely and do justice and righteousness in the land. In His days Judah will be saved, and Israel will dwell securely; and this is His name by which He will be called, 'The Lord our Righteousness'" (Jeremiah 23:5, 6).

This verse not only portrays the Messiah as David's son, reigning over the earth in the latter days and bringing peace, justice and righteousness, but it also calls him by a title reserved exclusively for God Himself—"Jehovah our Righteousness." This strongly indicates that the Messiah who would be a blood descendant of David and thus a man, would also be deity. The Jewish Targum Jonathan Ben Uzziel ascribes these same verses as referring to Messiah.

The second reason Solomon couldn't have fulfilled the prophecy of being the son of David referred to here is because Rabbis and Scribes of ancient times nearly all recognized and taught that this prophecy was speaking of the Messiah who would come in the latter days and rule Israel forever. Since Solomon died and ceased to reign on David's throne, that automatically disqualified him.

## JESUS PUTS THE SCRIBES ON THE HORNS OF A DILEMMA

Jesus once put a question to the theologians of his day concerning whose son the Messiah would be. These men all believed Messiah would be the son of David but evidently they hadn't thought through the implications of all the scriptures that dealt with that subject.

So, when they answered Jesus' question, "The Messiah will be the son of David," Jesus said to them, "Then how does David in the Spirit call Him [*David's son*] 'Lord,' saying, "THE LORD [*God*] SAID TO MY LORD [*David's son, Messiah*], "SIT AT MY RIGHT HAND, UNTIL I PUT THINE ENEMIES BENEATH THY FEET."' 'If David then calls Him 'Lord,' how is He his son?" (Matthew 22:41-45).

The explosive thrust of this paradoxical question was how David could call one of his sons 'Lord,' a title for God Himself, if his son was only a man.

Later, these same religious leaders were listening to Jesus speak and he saw them stoop down to pick up some stones to stone him. Jesus told them he had shown them many good works from the Father and he wondered which one they were stoning him for. Their answer was, "For a good work we do not stone you, but for blasphemy; and because you, being a man, make yourself out to be God" (John 10:31-33).

Later when they had put Jesus to trial on this same charge of blasphemy, the high priest put Jesus under oath and asked him, "Are you the Messiah, the Son of the Blessed One?" Jesus' answer was short and to the point, "I AM" (Mark 14:62a).

## DAVID'S 'GREATER SON' WAS THE CARPENTER FROM GALILEE

The clear witness of scripture is that a son of David would reign on David's throne forever and in Jesus' parentage he received the *royal* right to David's throne through his mother and the *regal* right through his step-father Joseph who were both of the line of David. He was the only living person in Israel who had the right to the throne of David and that's why God gave it to him.

After 70 C.E. when the temple was destroyed, all the birth-records were lost at that time. If someone had tried to make the claim of being Messiah, the son of David, after the year 70 C.E., there was no way he could prove it.

Whoever Messiah was, he had to have come before 70 C.E.!

A Prophet Like Moses

## DEUTERONOMY 18:18-19

"I will raise up a prophet from among their countrymen like you, and I will put My words in his mouth, and he shall speak to them all that I command him. And it shall come about that whoever will not listen to My words which he shall speak in My name, I Myself will require it of him."

נביא אקים להם מקרב אחיהם כמוך ונתתי דברי בפיו ודבר אליהם את כל-אשר אצונו : והיה האיש אשר לא- ישמע אל-דברי אשר ידבר בשמי אנכי אדרש מעמו :

## JOHN 5:45-47

"Do not think that I will accuse you before the Father; the one who accuses you is Moses, in whom you have set your hope. For if you believed Moses, you would believe Me; for he wrote of Me. But if you do not believe his writings, how will you believe My words?"

# A Prophet Like Moses

One of the most famous names of history is that of Moses, thanks to the Old Testament and Cecil B. De Mille's "The Ten Commandments." Moses almost didn't even make it out of infancy because he was one of the Hebrew children ordered murdered by Pharaoh when he became afraid that the Hebrew slaves were multiplying too quickly in the land of Egypt and might join with Egypt's enemies in case of a war.

God had plans for Moses, however, and he was miraculously saved from death and ended up being raised in Pharaoh's house as the adopted son of the sister of Pharaoh. At the age of 40, Moses was one of the mightiest and most educated men in Egypt and no doubt would have become Pharaoh if God hadn't forcefully removed him from his role of leadership in Egypt and sent him into the desert for 40 years to prepare him for the real mission in life that God had for him.

## MOSES GETS HIS TRAINING

Moses spent the first 40 years of his life thinking he was really *something.* Then God put him on the back-side of the desert with a bunch of unruly sheep for 40 years and convinced him that he was *nothing.* Now he was ready for the last 40 years of his life where he was going to find out that God was *everything.* During these last years he was used by God to lead the hordes of Jews out of national slavery in Egypt. He was a mighty worker of miracles. He received the Law of God, the Ten Commandments, from God on Mount Sinai and supervised the construction of the portable house of worship for the Jews, known as the tabernacle, which they used during their 40 years of exile in the Sinai wilderness. He made great predictions about things that God would do in the future and he was responsible for the writing of the first five books of the Old Testament known as the Pentateuch.

Moses was truly the greatest of the Hebrew prophets. The role of a prophet was to receive revelation from God and then declare and interpret God and His will to men. The fact that Moses was a prince among the prophets of God was evident by this statement of God, "Hear now My words: If there is a prophet among you, I the Lord shall make Myself known to him in a vision. I shall speak with him in a dream. Not so, with My servant Moses. He is faithful in all My household; with him I speak mouth to mouth, even openly, and not in dark sayings, and he beholds the form of the Lord. Why then were you not afraid to speak against My servant Moses" (Numbers 12:6-8).

In a postscript that the Spirit of the Lord inspired to be written about Moses after his death, we read, "Since then no prophet has risen in Israel like Moses, whom the Lord knew face to face, for all the signs and wonders which the Lord sent him to perform in the land of Egypt against Pharaoh, and his servants, and all his land, and for all the mighty power and for the great terror which Moses performed in the sight of all Israel" (Deuteronomy 34:10-12).

## A GREATER PROPHET THAN MOSES, YET TO COME

From these statements we can see that Moses was unique among all prophets, both those who came before and those who would follow him. Yet, God made a promise through Moses that of all the prophets who would come after him, there would be one *ideal* prophet, similar to Moses and yet obviously one of greater scope. In a unique way God would put His words in this prophet's mouth and he would speak to Israel all that God commanded him. This future prophet was given authority even above that of Moses, for God said that anyone who refused His word spoken through this prophet in the Lord's name, would be dealt with by God Himself (Deuteronomy 18:18, 19).

Some have taught about this prophecy that the term 'prophet' is used in these passages as a collective noun and doesn't speak of a single unique prophet, especially not one that could be construed as Messiah. It's obvious from the context that many prophets are anticipated in Israel in the interim between Moses and the great future prophet. But it's also clear that one ideal prophet is the main intent of Deuteronomy 18:15-19 and that he would be the embodiment of the greatness of all the prophets put together; the final climactic word from God.

Some of the ancient Rabbis saw Messiah as a prophet who would be greater than Moses. This is evident from the comment of Rabbi Levi Ben Gershon, "In fact the Messiah is such a prophet as it is stated in the Midrash on the verse: 'Behold My servant shall prosper' (Isaiah 52:13) ... 'Moses by the miracles which he wrought drew but a single nation to the worship of God, but the Messiah will draw all nations to the worship of God.' "

## THE JEWS WERE LOOKING FOR A PROPHET TO COME

The religious leaders of Jesus' day certainly were looking for this prophet like Moses to come. When John the Baptist burst upon the scene and began to speak with authority and demand repentance of the nation, the religious leaders sent a special inquisition team to interrogate him. The questions that they asked reflected vividly the thinking of that day, "And this is the witness of John, when the Jews sent to him priests and Levites from Jerusalem to ask him, 'Who are you?' And he confessed and did not deny and he confessed, 'I am not the Christ.' And they asked him, 'What then? Are you Elijah?' And he said, 'I am not.' 'Are you the Prophet?' And he answered, 'No' " (John 1:19-21).

From these questions we can see that the priests were looking for "the Prophet" but they weren't sure whether he would be the Messiah or a distinct personality who would prepare Messiah's way.

Jesus wasn't timid about telling people who he believed himself to be. On one occasion when he had healed a man on the Sab-bath and the Jewish leaders were hassling him about it, Jesus told them that if God's word was really in them and they really loved the Lord then they would have understood why he had healed the man on the Sabbath and would have seen that he, Jesus, had come from God as the promised Messiah. He really hit the nail on the head when he concluded with, "Do not think that I will accuse you before the Father; the one who accuses you is Moses, in whom you have set your hope. For if you believed Moses, you would believe me; for he wrote of me" (John 5:45, 46).

## JESUS QUALIFIED AS 'THE PROPHET WHO WAS TO COME'

This statement of Jesus can't be passed off lightly. He said that Moses had written about him. Now the only way Moses could have written about Jesus was if somehow Moses had foreseen Jesus. When he spoke these convicting words to his critics, Jesus must have had in mind only one statement of Moses in particular—the one in Deuteronomy 18:15-19 where Moses predicted the coming of a great prophet, for this is the only clear passage in all of Moses' writings that originated with him that specifically pointed to the Messiah.

John the Baptist faithfully bore witness to Jesus' qualifications to be the great and final prophet who would speak to men on behalf of God. He emphasized that Jesus had been sent from heaven by God and therefore he knew, better than any prophet who had ever lived, what God wanted said to men. Here's his statement about Jesus, "He who comes from above is above all, he who is of the earth is from the earth and speaks of the earth. He who comes from heaven is above all. What he has seen and heard, of that He bears witness: ... For He whom God has sent speaks the words of God ..." (John 3:31-34).

The writer of the letter to the Hebrews sums it up beautifully, "God, after He spoke long ago to the fathers in the prophets in many portions and in many ways, in these last days has spoken to us in His Son, whom He appointed heir of all things, through whom also He made the world" (Hebrews 1:1-2).

# Born in Bethlehem

**MICAH 5:2, 4, 5**

"But as for you, Bethlehem Ephrathah, too little to be among the clans of Judah, from you One will go forth for Me to be ruler in Israel. His goings forth are from long ago, from the days of eternity."

And He will arise and shepherd His flock in the strength of the Lord, in the majesty of the name of the Lord His God. And they will remain, because at that time He will be great to the ends of the earth. And this One will be our peace.

ואתה בית-לחם אפרתה צעיר להיות באלפי יהודה ממך לי יצא להיות מושל ביש-ראל ומוצאתיו מקדם מימי עולם:

ועמד ורעה בעז יהוה בגאון שם יהוה אלהיו וישבו כי-עתה יגדל עד-אפסי ארץ: והיה זה שלום

**MATTHEW 2:4-6**

And gathering together all the chief priests and scribes of the people, he (Herod) began to inquire of them where the Christ was to be born. And they said to him, "In Bethlehem of Judea, for so it has been written by the prophet, "And you, Bethlehem, land of Judah, are by no means least among the leaders of Judah; for out of you shall come forth a Ruler, who will shepherd My people Israel."

# Born in Bethlehem

Once a year, at Christmas, the world is given a meaningful reminder of the lengths that God will go to to keep a promise and fulfill prophecy to the letter.

The prophet Micah, a contemporary and friend of Isaiah, was used by God to add several strategic pieces to the jigsaw puzzle of Messianic prophecy which had been unfolding through the centuries of Jewish history. In the fifth chapter of his book, Micah records one of the most specific predictions about the coming Messiah. His birth place was to be in an obscure village in the province of Judea in Palestine; the city that King David had been born in, Bethlehem.

Among those scholars, both Jewish and Christian, who have accepted the concept of a personal Messiah, this passage has almost unanimously been understood as referring to the place out of which the Messiah would come. The ancient Targum Jonathan says of Micah's prophecy, "Out of thee Bethlehem shall Messiah go forth before me, to exercise dominion over Israel, Whose name has been spoken from of old from the day of eternity" (Micah 5: 2).

The modern Jewish standard authority for interpretation is the Soncino set of commentaries on the Old Testament. It says about this remarkable prediction, "This prophecy of the Messiah is comparable with the more famous 'shoot out of the stock of Jesse' prophecy of Isaiah 11:1. To hearten the people in their calamitous plight, Micah foretells the coming of one from Bethlehem (i.e. of the House of David) who, in the strength of the Lord, will restore Israel to their land and rule over them in God's name in abiding peace."

## WISEMEN SOUGHT HIM THEN AND STILL DO!

So widespread was the knowledge that this passage of scripture predicted the origin of the Messiah, that when the three Gentile wisemen, sometimes called Magi, came from Mesopotamia to the court of Herod seeking to find the birthplace of the Jewish Messiah, Herod called in the theologians of Israel. When he inquired of these Jewish leaders where their Messiah was to be born, without hesitation they said, "In Bethlehem of Judea; for so it has been written by the prophet," and then they went on to quote Micah's prophecy to Herod.

## ALL IN THE HANDS OF GOD

There's never been any question for 2000 years about where Jesus was born. Everyone knows it was Bethlehem. But the circumstances of how his mother got there just in time for him to be born are amazing indeed. Until just shortly before His birth, Mary was living in Nazareth, which was the hometown of Joseph and her. Four years prior to this the Roman ruler, Caesar Augustus decided to impose a special taxation on some of his conquered provinces. This was done by forcing a census to be taken of the people which required each of them to return to the city of their traditional ancestry.

The Jews resented the idea of a special tax, so they sent a commission clear to Rome to protest it since Quirinius, the local governor of Syria, didn't have the authority to settle the problem. Those were days of slow communication and travel. The commission finally failed and the Jews had to submit to the enrollment and taxation. By the time the official tax collectors had worked their way eastward, town by town, and province by province, exactly enough delay was caused, all in the natural course of events, so that when the enrollment was put in force in Judea, and Mary and Joseph were forced to go to their ancestral city, Bethlehem. The exact time had come to Mary for the birth of the baby Jesus.

Neither Mary nor Caesar nor the Roman tax collectors did the timing, nor were they in charge of affairs. The God who rules the world had His hand on the wheel, and He literally "moved the peoples of the world and timed everything to the very day, so that Mary and Joseph got to Bethlehem just in time for Jesus, the chosen Messiah, to be born in the right place, the place designated by the infallible finger of prophecy!"*

---

*Messiah in Both Testaments, Fred John Meldau, page 29.

## ISAIAH 7:14

"Therefore the Lord Himself will give you a sign: Behold, a virgin will be with child and bear a son, and she will call His name Immanuel."

לכן יתן אדני הוא לכם אות הנה העלמה הרה וילדת בן וקראת שמו עמנו אל:

## LUKE 1:30-35

And the angel said to her, "Do not be afraid, Mary; for you have found favor with God. And behold, you will conceive in your womb, and bear a son, and you shall name Him Jesus.

"He will be great, and will be called the Son of the Most High; and the Lord God will give Him the throne of His father David; and He will reign over the house of Jacob forever; and His kingdom will have no end."

And Mary said to the angel, "How can this be, since I am a virgin?" And the angel answered and said to her, "The Holy Spirit will come upon you, and the power of the Most High will overshadow you; and for that reason the holy offspring shall be called the Son of God."

Born of a Virgin

# Born of a Virgin

Perhaps the most disputed claim that the New Testament makes about Jesus is that he was born of a virgin according to Isaiah's prediction (Isaiah 7:14). It isn't his birth which is questioned. That was quite normal. But it's the matter of how he was *conceived* which is disputed. In the usual manner of conception, a sperm and ovum must unite to produce a child. In the case of Jesus, the scripture records that there was no sperm present to impregnate Mary. She was overshadowed by the Holy Spirit and life was generated in an ovum in her womb that became the child Jesus.

When you get right down to it, all life is a miracle. Sperm and ovum come into contact with each other constantly and yet life doesn't always result. These two agents have been put into test-tubes and as natural an environ as can be has been artificially produced, but no life results. That's because God alone is the author of life. If I believe in an all-powerful, sovereign God, who can do anything He chooses, then it's no big thing to believe that He could give life to an ovum in a woman's womb without the aid of a male sperm, and He Himself could uniquely be that child's Father.

## ISAIAH PREDICTED THE VIRGIN BIRTH

It's consistent with all the other supernatural phenomenon associated with the Promised Messiah, that his entrance into this world would also be in a unique manner. Isaiah predicted specifically that a virgin would have a son and his name would be called 'Immanuel.' That name means, *God is with us!* He also wrote to his nation, Israel, "For a child will be born to us, a Son will be given to us; and the government will rest on His shoulders; and His name will be called Wonderful, Counselor, Mighty God, Eternal Father, Prince of Peace" (Isaiah 9:6).

That child who would be called the Mighty God and the Eternal Father is the same child who would be born of a virgin in Bethlehem. And that virgin's child was none other than Messiah himself. At least one Talmudic source equates this prophecy of a virgin-born child with Messiah. In the Babylonian Talmud, Rabbi Huni in the name of Rabbi Ide and Rabbi Joshua said, "This man is the King Messiah of whom it is said in Psalm 2:7, 'This day have I begotten thee.' "

## WHEN IS A VIRGIN A VIRGIN?

There's no doubt that this prophecy is the most widely disputed of all the purported Messianic prophecies. The scholars who discredit this prophecy do so on the basis of the fact that the Hebrew word 'almah' which is translated into the English word 'virgin' can also be translated into the word 'maiden.' That's true. The term 'almah' may sometimes mean 'a young maiden' but it always means an *unmarried* young girl. About this Martin Luther said, "If a Jew or Christian can prove to me that in any passage of Scripture almah means 'a married woman,' I will give him a hundred florins...."*

Since the original purpose for this passage about a virgin bearing a son had to do with the promise of a *miraculous* sign being given to the House of Judah that her enemies would not over-run her, it would be an empty and meaningless sign if a *young maiden* was simply to give birth to a child, and especially an illegitimate child. Child-bearing happens every day to married women and unfortunately to unmarried young maidens also. However, it would indeed be a miraculous sign to the House of David if a *virgin* was to give birth to a child.

However much men may dispute Jesus' claim to be the fulfillment of Isaiah's prophecy of a virgin-born son, and say that there was no expectation of the Messiah coming from a virgin, the fact cannot be overlooked that 250 years before Jesus was born, the Hebrew translation of the Old Testament into Greek (the Septuagint) translates the word 'almah' into a Greek word, *parthenos*, which can *only* mean 'virgin.' *Those* Jewish scribes were looking for a *virgin*-born Messiah!

---

*E. W. Hengstenberg, "Christology of the Old Testament," Volume 1, p. 418.

**MALACHI 3:1**

"Behold, I am going to send My messenger, and he will clear the way before Me. And the Lord, whom you seek, will suddenly come to His temple; and the messenger of the covenant, in whom you delight, behold, He is coming," says the Lord of hosts.

הנני שלח מלאכי ופנה-דרך לפני ופתאם יבוא אל-היכלו האדון אשר-
אתם מבקשים ומלאך הברית אשר-אתם חפצים הנה-בא אמר יהוה
צבאות :

# The Voice in the Wilderness

**ISAIAH 40:3**

A voice is calling, "Clear the way for the Lord in the wilderness; make smooth in the desert a highway for our God."

קוֹל קוֹרֵא בַּמִּדְבָּר פַּנּוּ דֶּרֶךְ יְהוָה יַשְּׁרוּ בָּעֲרָבָה מְסִלָּה לֵאלֹהֵינוּ :

**MATTHEW 3:1-3**

Now in those days John the Baptist came, preaching in the wilderness of Judea, saying, "Repent, for the kingdom of heaven is at hand." For this is the one referred to by Isaiah the prophet, saying, "The voice of one crying in the wilderness, 'Make ready the way of the Lord, make His paths straight!'" Now John himself had a garment of camel's hair, and a leather belt about his waist; and his food was locusts and wild honey.

# The Voice in the Wilderness

It isn't easy to play 'second fiddle' to some famous person, but there was a man whom Isaiah and Malachi both predicted would come whose main job was to do just that. He was called 'A Voice in the Wilderness' by Isaiah and designated as the Lord's 'Messenger' by Malachi (Isaiah 40:3; Malachi 3:1). His job was to announce the coming of Messiah and to call the nation of Israel into repentance in preparation for his coming.

At the time that Malachi made this prediction of the coming of the Messiah and his forerunner, the Jews had lived through such struggling times that they had begun to lose hope of the coming of Messiah to deliver them. It was around 400 B.C.E. and the Jews were back in their land after their Babylonian captivity. But their worship of God had begun to deteriorate simply to external rituals and outward conformity. In the four chapters of his book, Malachi consistently called for a fresh response to God out of a sincere motive of love and repentance. Malachi's prophecies of the two coming 'messengers' of God were meant to stimulate and encourage the people to straighten up and begin looking expectantly to the future for their deliverer.

## NO MORE PROPHETS IN THE LAND

After Malachi passed from the scene, 400 years of silence followed where there were no more prophets in the land. The Jewish historian Josephus records that the people were aware that God had ceased to send prophets to them during this time. In the meantime, the external system of religion became more detailed and severe and instead of it producing the desired result of *more* godliness in the lives of the people, it only seemed to drive them into deeper despair of ever being able to be the kind of people God wanted them to be. By the time of Jesus' day, the average Jew on the street was not particularly excited about his relationship with God. It was just something that was a part of his everyday routine as far

as his outer behavior was concerned. Some were more conscientious than others about following the Laws of their religion, but few were living what you would call a joyous, spiritual life.

## THE VOICE OUT OF THE WILDERNESS

Suddenly, after 400 years of silence from God, Jesus' cousin, who came to be known as John the Baptist, burst onto the scene and began a whirlwind campaign to call the people out of their spiritual hypocrisy and into repentance in preparation for the Messiah and the Kingdom of God which was soon to come. He asked them to accept his baptism in the River Jordon as their sign of repentance and inward receptivity to God's message and messenger.

Immediately the religious authorities sent a delegation to check John out. They thought he might be the Messiah, but when they asked him if he was, he told them he wasn't. He was only the prophetic voice predicted by Isaiah, whose job it was going to be to prepare the way for the appearance of Messiah.

It's not hard to see why John and his message didn't go over too well with the religious authorities—the Pharisees, Scribes and Sadducees. They were one of his favorite targets as he undiplomatically blasted the externalism and emptiness of their religious profession. He warned them that no outward system of rituals or good deeds would help them one bit if their hearts were full of pride, intolerance and inconsistency, of all of which they were guilty.

## THE *OTHER* MESSENGER WHO WAS TO COME

In the two prophecies we're considering here, Isaiah 40:3 and Malachi 3:1, there are three main points that are being emphasized. First, a prophet with a fiery message of repentance will come to prepare the way for the coming of a *second* messenger. This second messenger spoken of is called 'the Lord, whom you seek,' by Malachi and could refer to none other than their long-sought Messiah. He's also referred to in Malachi 3:1 as the 'Messenger (angel) of the Covenant.'

Several ancient Jewish scholars saw the correlation between these two titles and made these comments; Rabbi Aben Ezra (1093-1167 C.E.) "The Lord [*referred to in Malachi's prophecy*] is both Divine Majesty and the Angel of the Covenant, for the sentence is doubled." Rabbi David Kimchi (1160-1235 C.E.) said of this passage, " 'The Lord' is King Messiah; He is also the Angel of the Covenant."

So, the first point is that a messenger would come to declare that the Messiah was about to appear and to urge the people to get their hearts ready.

The second emphasis is that the one, whose coming was being prepared for, was none other than the Lord God, Himself. The Lord, speaking through the prophet Malachi said, "Behold *I* am going to send *My* messenger and he will clear the way for *Me*. . . ." Isaiah confirmed this same point when he wrote, "A voice is calling, clear the way for the *Lord* in the wilderness; Make smooth in the desert a highway for our *God.*"

The third thing to be noted in Malachi 3:1 is that after the messenger prepares the way for the coming of the Lord and He comes, He will go suddenly to *His* temple. Now, in order for the Lord to go to His temple, there must be a temple standing there for Him to go to. Since the year 70 C.E., the year Titus destroyed Jerusalem, there has been no Jewish temple. Therefore, it seems reasonable to conclude that whoever this Messenger of the Covenant (also referred to as *Lord, God* and *Messiah* by the prophets and scholars) was, he would have to have come before the year 70 C.E.

## WILL THE REAL ELIJAH PLEASE STAND UP?

Many people through history have connected Malachi's prophecy of a forerunner with another prophecy he also made, "Behold, I am going to send you Elijah the prophet before the coming of the great and terrible day of the Lord" (Malachi 4:5).

From this they concluded that any forerunner who would herald the Messiah's coming would have to be Elijah himself. If you'll remember, the religious interrogators of John the Baptist asked him if he was Elijah and he said "No."

Jesus' disciples posed a similar question to him about Elijah, ". . . 'Why then do the scribes say that Elijah must first come?' Jesus answered and said, 'Elijah is coming and will restore all things; but I say to you that Elijah already came and they did not recognize him, but did to him whatever they wished' " (Matthew 17:10-12). Note that Jesus specifically says that Elijah *is coming* (future) and will restore all things. But he also emphasized that Elijah *had already come* and wasn't recognized in his role as forerunner of Messiah. What he meant by this was that John the Baptist, who heralded Jesus' coming with such power and conviction, was a 'type' of Elijah and was counted by God as a fulfillment of Malachi's prophecy that Elijah was coming before the great day of the Lord. Jesus told his disciples, "If you care to accept it, he (John the Baptist) is Elijah, who was to come" (Matthew 11:14).

## A CASE OF DIVINE FOREKNOWLEDGE

This seeming problem is solved by realizing that God foreknew that Israel would reject Messiah in his role as the Servant of the Lord, suffering for the sins of the people. Nevertheless, he sent John as a *type* of Elijah to prepare the way for the Kingdom and the King Messiah. Had they accepted Jesus as Messiah, the Kingdom of God would have become a reality and John would have qualified as Elijah.

It must be made clear, however, that Elijah, in person, is still going to come. Since Jesus was rejected as Messiah when he came 20 centuries ago, he's going to come again, this time as a stern judge and conquering King who will put down all unrighteousness and establish the Kingdom of God on this earth. Elijah will personally herald that coming and that's the day the Nation of Israel will "look on Him whom they have pierced" (Zechariah 12:10) and realize that he's the same person who came to them 2000 years ago as their Messiah.

# The Anointing of the Spirit

### ISAIAH 42:1

"Behold, My Servant, whom I uphold; My chosen one in whom My soul delights. I have put My Spirit upon Him; He will bring forth justice to the nations.

הן עבדי אתמך-בו בחירי רצתה נפשי נתתי רוחי עליו משפט לגוים יוציא:

### LUKE 3:21-22

Now it came about when all the people were baptized, that Jesus also was baptized, and while He was praying, heaven was opened, and the Holy Spirit descended upon Him in bodily form like a dove, and a voice came out of heaven, "Thou are My Beloved Son, in Thee I am well-pleased."

# The Anointing of the Spirit

Over 2700 years ago, the eloquent prophet Isaiah gave us a beautiful verbal portrait of what a truly Spirit-filled man would be like, when he predicted the *character* of the Messiah as the Spirit of the Lord would come to rest on him:

> "And the Spirit of the LORD will
> rest on Him,
>
> The spirit of *wisdom* and *understanding*,
> The spirit of *counsel* and *strength*,
> The spirit of *knowledge* and the
> *fear of the LORD*.
> And He will *delight* in the fear of
> the LORD,
> And He will not judge by what
> His eyes see,
> Nor make a decision by what
> His ears hear;
> But with *righteousness* He will
> judge the poor,
> And decide with *fairness* for the
> afflicted of the earth;
> And He will strike the earth with the
> rod of His mouth,
> And with the breath of His lips He will
> slay the wicked.
> Also *righteousness* will be the belt
> about His loins,
> And *faithfulness* the belt
> about His waist" (Isaiah 11:2-5).

A little later in Isaiah's prophecies the Lord speaks of this lovely person again as He says through Isaiah, "Behold, My Servant, whom I uphold; My chosen one in whom My soul delights. I have put My Spirit upon him; He will bring forth justice to the nations.

## WHO IS THE SERVANT?

Jewish commentators on this passage are divided between whether the Servant refers to Israel, Messiah or the prophet Isaiah himself. I agree with Rabbi Isaac Ben Judah Abrabanel (1437-1508 C.E.) who said of the Jewish sages who didn't see Messiah in this verse, "All these expositors were struck with blindness."* There is no nation or human

---

*E. W. Hengstenberg, *Christology of the Old Testament*, p. 530.

being who could fulfill all the exploits this Spirit-anointed Servant is said to do. Just one that I'll mention would take God Himself to fulfill. Isaiah said of this Servant, "He will faithfully bring forth justice. He will not be disheartened or crushed, until He has established justice in the [whole] earth" (Isaiah 42:3b-4a). That's a job for Messiah and one which the prophets consistently said that he alone would do.

## THE ANOINTING OF JESUS

At the beginning of Jesus' public ministry, he went out to the Jordan River where John was baptizing men and women. In presenting himself to be baptized, he was really presenting himself to the Father as being available and ready to start the ministry the Father had for him to do. As he stepped into the water, he was immersing himself into total submission to the Father's will, a will which Jesus knew would take him to the cross, bearing the sins of mankind.

The Father immediately responded to this yielded spirit by sending upon him the Holy Spirit in the visible form of a dove. God also gave a verbal acceptance for everyone to hear, "Thou art My beloved Son, in Thee I am well pleased" (Luke 3:22). These words of commendation are the same thoughts found in Isaiah 41:1, "My chosen one in whom My soul delights."

Jesus was aware of the fact that he was the Anointed Servant that Isaiah had predicted. This is evident from an incident that occurred in the synagogue. "And the book of the prophet Isaiah was handed to Him (Jesus). And He opened the book and found the place where it is written, 'The Spirit of the Lord is upon Me, because He has anointed Me to preach the Gospel to the poor. He has sent Me to proclaim release to the captives, and recovery of sight to the blind, to set free those who are downtrodden, to proclaim the favorable year of the Lord.'

And He closed the book and gave it back to the attendant and sat down; and the eyes of all in the Synagogue were fixed upon Him. And He began to say to them, 'Today this Scripture has been fulfilled in your hearing' " (Luke 4:17-21).

And you could have heard a pin drop!

## ISAIAH 35:4-6

Say to those with palpitating heart, "Take courage, fear not. Behold, your God will come with vengeance; the recompense of God will come, but He will save you."

Then the eyes of the blind will be opened, and the ears of the deaf will be unstopped. Then the lame will leap like a deer, and the tongue of the dumb will shout for joy. For waters will break forth in the wilderness and streams in the Arabah.

אמרו לנמהרי־לב חזקו אל־תיראו הנה אלהיכם נקם יבוא גמול אלהים הוא יבוא וישעכם:

אז תפקחנה עיני עורים ואזני חרשים תפתחנה: אז ידלג כאיל פסח ותרן לשון אלם כי־נבקעו במדבר מים ונחלים בערבה:

## MATTHEW 11:2-6

Now when John in prison heard of the works of Christ, he sent word by his disciples, and said to Him, "Are You the Coming One, or shall we look for someone else?"

And Jesus answered and said to them, "Go and report to John the things which you hear and see: the blind receive sight and the lame walk, the lepers are cleansed and the deaf hear, and the dead are raised up, and the poor have the gospel preached to them. And blessed is he who keeps from stumbling over Me."

Miracles of Healing

# Miracles of Healing

At any period of history one who can work genuine miracles has been a phenomenon. During their long history, the nation of Israel saw many miracle workers, even though they weren't all from God. However, during the 400 years when the prophets had ceased to speak to the nation, miracles had pretty much died out and so-called miracle workers fell on hard times.

But Isaiah the prophet had predicted that the phenomenon of miracles would be revived and reach a new height when Messiah came. He not only said that the Promised One would bring physical healing to the afflicted, but he would heal the arid land too. The blind would see, the deaf hear, the lame and crippled would leap like young deer, the dumb would burst forth in songs of praise and streams would flow in the desert (Isaiah 35:4-6).

These miracles of healing were to be the credentials by which the Messiah could authenticate himself as being genuine. The miracles would prove that "the Spirit of the Lord was upon him" and that "he was anointed to bind up the broken hearted, and set at liberty the captives of sin" (Isaiah 42:1; 61:1-2).

## JESUS STRAIGHTENS JOHN OUT

While John the Baptist was lying in Herod's dungeon for having condemned Herod's marriage to his brother's wife, he got to thinking about all the prophecies that were to be fulfilled by Messiah when he came. He knew that Messiah was supposed to purify his people and destroy those who oppressed and persecuted the people of God. But he also knew Messiah was to suffer for the redemption of Israel as well as all mankind, for John himself had said of Jesus earlier, "Behold the lamb of God who takes away the sin of the world" (John 1:29).

But as John lay there in prison trying to see how one man could fulfill *both* of these roles, he decided to send someone to ask Jesus himself who he really was. So, some of his disciples went to Jesus and asked, " 'Are you the Coming One, or shall we look for someone else?' Jesus answered them, 'Go and report to John the things which you hear and see: the BLIND RECEIVE SIGHT and the LAME WALK, the LEPERS ARE CLEANSED and the DEAF HEAR, and the DEAD ARE RAISED UP, and the POOR HAVE THE GOSPEL PREACHED TO THEM. And blessed is he who keeps from stumbling over me' " (Matthew 11:2-6).

Jesus took it for granted that John knew these predictions about Messiah's miraculous powers and he knew that just to quote these prophecies to John would reassure him of who he really was. He didn't try to explain the seemingly paradoxical problem of how he was going to fulfill both portraits of the Messiah, the Suffering One and the Kingly One. He merely set forth his miracles as totally sufficient credentials that he was Messiah, the Coming One that John was looking for.

## THE UNPARDONABLE SIN

The spiritual blindness Jesus faced was sometimes overwhelming. One day a demon-possessed man who was blind and dumb was healed by Jesus, and the people who witnessed it began to say among themselves, "Wow! Maybe this is the Son of David, the Messiah we've been looking for, since he's done this incredible miracle." But when the Pharisees heard about it, they said that Jesus cast out demons in the power of Satan (Matthew 12:22-24 paraphrased).

In response to this, Jesus issued the most solemn warning of his whole ministry, ". . . any sin and blasphemy shall be forgiven men; but blasphemy against the Spirit shall not be forgiven. And whoever shall speak a word against the Son of Man, it shall be forgiven him; but whoever shall speak against the Holy Spirit, it shall not be forgiven him, either in this age or in the age to come" (Matthew 12:3-32).

These religious bigots knew the prophecies that the Messiah was to be anointed with the Spirit and given the power to perform miracles by him. Yet when they saw a man who claimed to be Messiah and was authenticating it with these very predicted signs and then they attributed the source of those miracles to Satan, there was no pardon for that kind of unbelief.

**ZECHARIAH 9:9**

Rejoice greatly, O daughter of Zion! Shout in triumph, O daughter of Jerusalem! Behold, your king is coming to you; He is just and endowed with salvation, humble, and mounted on a donkey, even on a colt, the foal of a donkey.

גִּילִי מְאֹד בַּת־צִיּוֹן הָרִיעִי בַּת יְרוּשָׁלִַם הִנֵּה מַלְכֵּךְ יָבוֹא לָךְ צַדִּיק וְנוֹשָׁע הוּא עָנִי וְרֹכֵב עַל־חֲמוֹר וְעַל־עַיִר בֶּן־אֲתֹנוֹת :

And the disciples went and did just as Jesus had directed them, and brought the donkey and the colt, and laid on them their garments, on which He sat. And most of the multitude spread their garments in the road, and others were cutting branches from the trees, and spreading them in the road.

And the multitudes going before Him, and those who followed after were crying out, saying, "Hosanna to the Son of David; blessed is He who comes in the name of the Lord; hosanna in the highest!"

# The Official Presentation

# The Official Presentation

The entrance of Jesus into Jerusalem with his followers wildly proclaiming him as King Messiah is usually referred to by Christian theologians as 'The Triumphal Entry.' If it was a triumph, however, it was very shortlived for within one week he was hanging dead on a cross above this same city of Jerusalem.

What went wrong with the disciples' expectation that Jesus, as Messiah, was on the verge of setting up the Kingdom of God and liberating the Jews from the tyranny of Rome?

Nothing went wrong as far as God's plans were concerned. The problem was that no one had really tuned in on the things that Jesus had been saying about why he had really come. For instance, Jesus had told his disciples that he had come to seek and to save the lost, and by that he meant those who were sinners (Luke 19:10). But later, when he was trying to prepare his disciples for the events that would be involved in his doing that, he told them that he would have to go to Jerusalem and suffer many things from the religious leaders and be killed, but that he would rise again on the third day. Then Peter, speaking for the group and manifesting a total lack of understanding about what Jesus had just said, took him aside and began to rebuke him, saying, "God forbid it, Lord! This shall never happen to you" (Matthew 16:21, 22 paraphrased).

## THE PIECES BEGIN TO FALL IN PLACE

It was not until after the death and resur-rection of Jesus that his followers began to put all the pieces together and saw what he had been trying to say to them all along. There were two distinct roles that Messiah was predicted to fulfill in his coming; one to bear the sins of men and reconcile them to God and the other was to bring the King-dom of God, that long-awaited era of peace and prosperity, to Israel and the world. Both of these could be accomplished by one person, King Messiah, but *not* at the same time. First, Messiah would have to deal with the root of men's problem, a nature and heart of rebellion and sin, and *then* he could set up a Kingdom where all men would be prepared to live at peace with themselves, their families and their neighbors. But until the first was accomplished, the second could only be a dream, never a reality.

Unfortunately, men don't like to be re-minded that they're sinful and when this became the emphasis of Jesus' teaching and he never got around to gathering an army and setting up plans for overthrowing the government and taking the throne of David, many people became disillusioned with him as a candidate for Messiah. Since they didn't want to admit that sinful *motives* were as bad as sinful *actions*, they began to resent Jesus' continual emphasis on their needing to repent and come to him for for-giveness.

## THE PUZZLE OF THE TWO PORTRAITS OF MESSIAH

In one sense, it's easy to see how they were confused about Jesus and his claim to be

Messiah. The Old Testament seemed to predict two very contradictory pictures of Messiah. One showed him as coming from the family of King David, rising from obscurity into national prominence, destroying all the enemies of Israel and setting up a kingdom of universal peace, both politically and spiritually. The Jewish people were to be appointed as political and spiritual leaders in the kingdom. Such a picture fit in well with the nationalistic hopes of the Jews suffering under the iron-fisted oppression of the Roman Empire.

The other picture of the Messiah which emerged from the prophecies in the Old Testament was that of a humble, gentle servant who would teach patiently, but would suffer and die for the sins of his people. He would be rejected by his own countrymen as well as hated by other peoples. This picture of Messiah is sometimes called 'The Suffering Messiah' and Isaiah speaks much about him.

Before Jesus lived on this earth, the two pictures were confusing to students of prophecy. They grasped the two roles of Messiah clearly but the connection between them escaped the most brilliant of interpreters. How could one man have such contradictory aspects? Most Jewish scholars just left the problem of how to harmonize these two roles to be solved by any future prophets who might come.

Other commentators invented a theory that perhaps *two* Messiahs were meant to come. The conquering King would be the Son of David and the suffering, lowly one would be in the tradition of Joseph, the Jewish lad who had suffered so badly at the hands of his brothers by being sold into slavery in Egypt and then had risen to prominence there. This Messiah began to be referred to as Messiah ben Joseph.*

What all these learned men failed to see was that *all* the predictions of Messiah, both concepts of him, were to be fulfilled in one man, but not at one time. There was to be a period of time in between the two roles he would play and that would necessitate that he appear on the earth at two different times. The prophets themselves, who wrote

*Encyclopaedia Judaica, *Messiah*, page 1414.

these seemingly contradictory predictions, didn't understand this concept either. To them, as they looked down the corridors of history, the coming of Messiah in these two roles was like two great mountain peaks in the distance. What they couldn't see, however, was that in between these two peaks there was a valley—a valley of time which has now lasted nearly 2000 years. The first peak represented Messiah's *first* coming as the Lamb of God and Savior of men's souls, while the second peak would represent his *second* coming as the Lion of Judah to establish the Kingdom of God on earth.

## THE 'REAL' TRIUMPH OF JESUS' ENTRANCE

When Jesus rode into Jerusalem on a donkey's foal, he was fully aware that this was fulfilling Zechariah's prediction of what the Messiah would do. Zechariah had told the people that when Messiah came to them, riding on a donkey, they would 're-joice greatly and shout in triumph for their king was coming to them endowed with salvation' (9:9). Jesus also knew that the cries of enthusiasm would soon die out as he went through what was going to be necessary for their salvation to become a reality. Nevertheless, when the infuriated and frightened religious leaders saw the ecstatic throngs following Jesus with palm leaves ready to crown him king, right on the spot, they shouted to Jesus for him to rebuke his disciples and to stop the whole procedure.

But Jesus' answer to them is one of the most classic statements in the entire word of God. He said to them, "I tell you, if these people were to become silent and fail to proclaim me as the Messiah, predicted and looked for through centuries past, these very stones on which I'm riding and in the walls of this great city would cry out, '*Blessed is He who comes in the name of the Lord*', for *this very day* is the day of Israel's salvation' " (literal paraphrase of Luke 19:38-42).

And as he looked across the faces of the multitudes, knowing that most of them would reject that salvation, he broke into sobs and said, "If you had only known in this day the things which make for your peace! But now they have been hidden from your eyes" (Luke 19:42 paraphrase).

## Prophecy of Betrayal

**PSALM 41:9**

Even my close friend, in whom I trusted, who ate my bread, has lifted up his heel against me.

גַּם-אִישׁ שְׁלוֹמִי אֲשֶׁר-בָּטַחְתִּי בוֹ אוֹכֵל לַחְמִי הִגְדִּיל עָלַי עָקֵב:

**JOHN 13:18, 21, 26**

"I do not speak of all of you. I know the ones I have chosen; but it is that the Scripture may be fulfilled, 'He who eats My bread has lifted up his heel against Me.'"

. . .

When Jesus had said this, He became troubled in spirit, and testified, and said, "Truly, truly, I say to you, that one of you will betray Me."

. . .

Jesus therefore answered, "That is the one for whom I shall dip the morsel and give it to him." So when He had dipped the morsel, He took and gave it to Judas, the son of Simon Iscariot.

# Prophecy of Betrayal

In Israel's religious calendar, the Feast of the Passover has been one of the most important celebrations in their national history. For over 2700 years it's been a continuous yearly festival commemorating the deliverance of the children of Israel out of bondage in Egypt. Every Jew who was able to do so tried to make it to Jerusalem for the Passover celebration in the Temple itself. Josephus, the Jewish historian, estimated that in 65 C.E. just five years before the Second Temple (the one of Jesus' time) was destroyed by Titus, over three million Jews were in Jerusalem to celebrate Passover.*

The Passover festivities took seven days to complete but always began with the traditional meal on the first night where each family took a lamb and killed it, sprinkling the blood on the doorpost, and then ate it with unleavened bread and bitter herbs.

This meal today is called the Seder meal but during the last week of Jesus' life, he ate this traditional supper with his disciples in order to prepare them for his soon coming death. Because it was his last Passover meal, the New Testament writers have called it 'The Last Supper.'

## JESUS PREDICTED HIS COMING DEATH

On several occasions during his ministry, Jesus clearly spoke to his disciples about the events that would close out his earthly career and bring about his death. At one point he said, "The Son of Man is to be betrayed into the hands of men, and they will kill Him, and when He has been killed, He will rise again three days later. But they did not understand this statement, and they were afraid to ask Him" (Mark 9:31, 32).

Now, at the Passover meal he was going to explain in detail what he had predicted earlier about his betrayal and coming death. He said, "From now on I am telling you before it comes to pass, so that when it does occur, you may believe that I am He

*Encyclopaedia Judaica, *Passover*, page 164.

[Messiah]" (John 13:19). In other words, he was hazarding his whole Messianic credibility on whether he would rise from the dead on the third day as he was predicting.

## BETRAYED BY A FRIEND

Naturally, the mood of the Last Supper was not a happy one as it might have been on other Passover celebrations. They were grieved at the thought that Jesus felt that he was going to be killed. They all lived with a certain amount of danger just being one of his disciples but it was quite another thing for Jesus to say with certainty that he was definitely going to be killed within days.

But their greatest shock came while they were sitting at the table and Jesus calmly said, "I know the ones I have chosen; but it is that the Scriptures may be fulfilled, 'He who eats My bread has lifted up his heel against me' (Psalm 41:9).... When Jesus had said this, He became troubled in spirit, and testified and said, 'Truly, truly, I say to you, that one of you will betray me' " (John 13:18, 21). Jesus was revealing here that a prophecy made over 1000 years before in Psalm 41:9 about King David's friend betraying him at a meal, was actually going to happen to him (Jesus) thus confirming it as a Messianic prophecy.

At this point, John privately asked Jesus who it was that would betray him. Jesus told him that it was the one to whom he would give the 'sop.' This must have flabbergasted John, because the 'sop,' which consisted of the best piece of the Passover lamb and a piece of unleavened bread with herbs, was only given to the *most honored guest* at the supper.

In this gracious act of Jesus we can see that he loved his betrayer, Judas, to the end. This gesture of honoring him was Jesus' final attempt to woo his heart and cause him to repent and put his trust in Jesus as Messiah. This prediction of Judas' betrayal also shows that Jesus knew it was going to happen but he did nothing to stop it. He knew it was all part of his Father's ultimate plan for the redemption of Israel and all mankind.

# Betrayed For Thirty Pieces of Silver

**ZECHARIAH 11:12**

And I said to them, "If it is good in your sight, give me my wages; but if not, never mind!" So they weighed out thirty shekels of silver as my wages.

וָאֹמַר אֲלֵיהֶם אִם־טוֹב בְּעֵינֵיכֶם הָבוּ שְׂכָרִי וְאִם־לֹא חֲדָלוּ וַיִּשְׁקְלוּ אֶת־שְׂכָרִי שְׁלֹשִׁים כָּסֶף׃

**MATTHEW 26:14-15**

Then one of the twelve, named Judas Iscariot, went to the chief priests, and said, "What are you willing to give me to deliver Him up to you?" And they weighed out to him thirty pieces of silver.

**ZECHARIAH 11:13**

Then the Lord said to me, "Throw it to the potter, that magnificent price at which I was valued by them." So I took the thirty shekels of silver and threw them to the potter in the house of the Lord.

ויאמר יהוה אלי השליכהו אל-היוצר אדר היקר אשר יקרתי מעליהם ואקחה שלשים הכסף ואשליך אתו בית יהוה אל-היוצר :

**MATTHEW 27:3-7**

Then when Judas, who had betrayed Him, saw that He had been condemned, he felt remorse and returned the thirty pieces of silver to the chief priests and elders, saying, "I have sinned by betraying innocent blood. " But they said, "What is that to us? See to that yourself!"

And he threw the pieces of silver into the sanctuary and departed; and he went away and hanged himself. And the chief priests took the pieces of silver and said, "It is not lawful to put them into the temple treasury, since it is the price of blood." And they counseled together and with the money bought the Potter's Field as a burial place for strangers.

Silver Cast Down In Temple

# Betrayed For Thirty Pieces of Silver

As Judas Iscariot approached the High Priest of Israel with his offer to betray Jesus to him, he had no idea that because of his own spiritual blindness he was acting out a drama of infamy that had been predicted some 550 years before by the prophet Zechariah.

As the Passover season was approaching and Jesus and his disciples made their plans to be in Jerusalem for the celebration, Judas, for reasons known only to his own tortured mind, determined that this would be the best time to betray Jesus.

No one can say for sure why Judas, who had been Jesus' disciple and companion for nearly three years, would now decide to turn him over to the religious authorities. Some have theorized that Judas' main attraction to Jesus had been in his ardent hope that Jesus was the long-awaited Son of David who would deliver the nation of Israel from the Roman tyrants.

Judas had joined with Jesus and his band at the beginning, when the multitudes were following Jesus everywhere and hanging on his every word. But, step by step he had become disillusioned with what he had thought were Jesus' aspirations to take over the government and set up a Jewish Kingdom of God. John the Baptist had been beheaded and Jesus hadn't avenged him. In fact, he'd withdrawn himself from the public for awhile. It seemed to Judas that Jesus was more and more refusing to face his opposition and there was no question but what the opposition to Jesus was rapidly growing. More and more Jesus was telling his disciples to be ready for the shame and possible death that might be associated with being a follower of him. What could all this mean to Judas except that he had been mis-

taken in his dream of rising into power at the side of the new King of Israel!

## 30 INFAMOUS PIECES OF SILVER

Whatever the motives were that led Judas to the point of betrayal, he was fitting into the unfolding drama that would soon put Jesus on a Roman cross. When Judas went to the chief priests and asked them, "What are you willing to give me to deliver Jesus up to you?", the *priests* came up with the figure of 30 pieces of silver (Matthew 26:14-16).

The arrival at that specific amount of money was no chance happening. Five-hundred years before, Zechariah had predicted that there would come a time when the nation of Israel would estimate the value of their God at 30 pieces of silver! It would be at a time in the nation's history when because of sin and unbelief, God would remove His protective hand from them and allow the nations to slaughter and take into captivity His covenant people. Since this prediction was made *after* their Babylonian captivity had ended and nothing like it had happened till the time of Jesus, it could only have been referring prophetically to the holocaust of 70 C.E. when Titus destroyed Jerusalem and slaughtered hundreds of thousands of Jews and took many more captive.

The God of Israel, speaking through the prophet Zechariah, predicted His rejection by the people at that time in this way, " 'If it is good in your sight, give me my wages; but if not, never mind!' So they weighed out thirty shekels of silver as my wages" ... "that magnificent price at which I was valued by them" (Zechariah 11:12, 13a).

It's very unlikely that the priests who set

the sum of 30 pieces of silver even faintly connected Zechariah's words with what they were doing. To them, no doubt, the figure of 30 shekels was meant to show their derision of Jesus since that was the official value of a slave (Exodus 21:32).

But to me, the greatest significance of what they did was that the money they gave to Judas for Jesus' betrayal was taken out of the Temple treasury which was where the money was kept to buy the sacrifices used in the Temple services. It was with these sacrifices that the priests made the blood offerings for the sins of the people. Little did they realize the implications of this 'sacrifice' which they were purchasing.

## JUDAS HAS SECOND THOUGHTS!

Judas didn't hate Jesus and he really didn't wish him any bodily harm. No doubt he thought that the Sanhedrin, the ruling body of Jewish leaders, would perhaps severely rebuke Jesus and forcefully nip-in-the-bud his aspirations of becoming Messiah, since Judas no longer believed that he was. However, Judas didn't reckon on the nature of the threat that Jesus was to the institutionalized religion of Judaism and the insane hatred that he had invoked among the religious hierarchy.

When he saw Jesus being taken through a series of sober trials, whipped and badly beaten and then sentenced to death, he felt great remorse about what he'd done because he hadn't counted on it going this far. He had to try to stop this awful nightmare before it actually resulted in Jesus' death. No doubt he felt that if he returned the money to the priests and confessed to them that he had betrayed an innocent man, they would call off their accusations of Jesus and release him.

Judas ran in a frenzy to the temple, seeking the chief priests and elders and when he found them he blurted out, "I have sinned by betraying innocent blood." Now, normally when priests or Rabbis find a penitent man in front of them confessing that he's sinned, they take it a little more seriously than the case was here. Their response to Judas was, "So what! What's that to us? That's your problem" (paraphrase of Matthew 27:4). Since they were cohorts

with Judas in the sin of betraying an innocent man, there wasn't much they could say or do to Judas without condemning themselves.

## SILVER CAST DOWN IN TEMPLE

Not knowing where to turn or what to do at this point, Judas ran headlong toward the Sanctuary of the Temple itself, and thinking to purge himself of the awful treachery he'd done, he threw the money into the House of the Lord and ran off and hung himself.

Listen to Zechariah's description of this event five centuries *before* it happened, "... the thirty shekels of silver were *thrown* ... into the house of the Lord" (Zechariah 11:13). The only concern that this gave the priests was that now they had to decide what to do with the money. It wasn't lawful for them to put unlawfully gained money into the Temple treasury to use for the purchase of sacred things. If donations of this sort were made to the Temple, it was supposed to be returned to the donor. But if he insisted on giving it, then the money had to be spent for something for the public good.*

This seemingly insignificant Rabbinic law brought about the detailed fulfillment of the last part of Zechariah's remarkable prophecy. He had said that the 30 shekels of silver would be given to the 'potter' after they were thrown into the House of the Lord. Here's how the priests handled this 'sticky' problem: "And they counseled together and with the money bought the Potter's Field as a burial place for strangers" (Matthew 27:7).

The 'Potter's Field' was located on the exact spot where the Prophet Jeremiah had so long before divinely prophesied against the sinfulness of Jerusalem and all Israel. And now that sinfulness had reached its epitomy in the rejection of the Messiah. How tragically ironic that the money gained by betraying that Messiah should be used to buy Jeremiah's field, thus validating all the indictments he had made concerning the spiritual insensitivity and blindness of the nation of Israel.*

---

*Edersheim, *The Life and Times of Jesus the Messiah*, Vol. 2, page 575.

# Of Whom Does the Prophet Speak?

## ISAIAH 53

*The Servant's Exaltation Through Humiliation.* Behold, my servant shall prosper, he shall be exalted and lifted up, and shall be very high. As many were astonished at him—his appearance was so marred, beyond human semblance, and his form beyond that of the sons of men—so shall he startle (sprinkle) many nations; kings shall shut their mouths because of him! for that which has not been told them they shall see, and that which they have not heard they shall understand.

*The Servant as Seen by Man: Despised and Rejected.* Who has believed what we have heard? And to whom has the arm of the LORD been revealed? For he grew up before him like a young plant, and like a root out of dry ground; he had no form or comeliness that we should desire him. He was despised and rejected by men; a man of sorrows and acquainted with grief, and as one from whom men hide their faces he was despised, and we esteemed him not.

*The Servant as Seen by God: the Redeemer.* Surely he has borne our griefs and carried our sorrows; yet we esteemed him stricken, smitten by God, and afflicted. But he was wounded for our transgressions, he was bruised for our iniquities; upon him was the chastisement that made us whole, and with his stripes we are healed. All we like sheep have gone astray; we have turned every one to his own way; and the LORD has laid on him the iniquity of us all.

*His Death as Seen by Man: Tragic Failure.* He was oppressed and he was afflicted, yet he opened not his mouth; like a lamb that is led to the slaughter, and like a sheep that before its shearers is dumb, so he opened not his mouth. By oppression and judgment he was taken away; and as for his generation, who considered that he was cut off out of the land of the living, stricken for the transgression of my people? And they made his grave with the wicked and with a rich man in his death, although he had done no violence, and there was no deceit in his mouth.

*His Death as Seen by God: Glorious Success.* Yet it was the will of the LORD to bruise him; he has put him to grief; when he makes himself an offering for sin, he shall see his offspring, he shall prolong his days; the will of the LORD shall prosper in his hand; he shall see the fruit of the travail of his soul and be satisfied; by his knowledge shall the righteous one, my servant, make many to be accounted righteous; and he shall bear their iniquities. Therefore I will divide him a portion with the great, and he shall divide the spoil with the strong; because he poured out his soul to death, and was numbered with the transgressors; yet he bore the sin of many, and made intercession for the transgressors. (*RSV*)

הנה ישכיל עבדי ירום ונשא וגבה מאד : כאשר שממו עליך רבים כן-משחת
מאיש מראהו ותארו מבני אדם : כן יזה גוים רבים עליו יקפצו מלכים פיהם כי
אשר לא-ספר להם ראו ואשר לא-שמעו התבוננו :

מי האמין לשמעתנו וזרוע יהוה על-מי נגלתה : ויעל כיונק לפניו וכשרש מארץ
ציה לא-תאר לו ולא הדר ונראהו ולא מראה ונחמדהו : נבזה וחדל אישים איש
מכאבות וידוע חלי וכמסתר פנים ממנו נבזה ולא חשבנהו :

אכן חלינו הוא נשא ומכאבינו סבלם ואנחנו חשבנהו נגוע מכה אלהים ומענה :
והוא מחלל מפשענו מדכא מעונתינו מוסר שלומנו עליו ובחברתו נרפא-לנו :
כלנו כצאן תעינו איש לדרכו פנינו ויהוה הפגיע בו את עון כלנו :

נגש והוא נענה ולא יפתח-פיו כשה לטבח יובל וכרחל לפני גזיה נאלמה ולא יפתח
פיו : מעצר וממשפט לקח ואת-דורו מי ישוחח כי נגזר מארץ חיים מפשע עמי
נגע למו : ויתן את-רשעים קברו ואת-עשיר במתיו על לא-חמס עשה ולא מרמה
בפיו :

ויהוה חפץ דכאו החלי אם-תשים אשם נפשו יראה זרע יאריך ימים וחפץ יהוה בידו
יצלח : מעמל נפשו יראה ישבע בדעתו יצדיק צדיק עבדי לרבים ועונתם הוא
יסבל : לכן אחלק-לו ברבים ואת-עצומים יחלק שלל תחת אשר הערה למות נפשו
ואת-פשעים נמנה והוא חטא-רבים נשא ולפשעים יפגיע :

## ISAIAH 53:7

He was oppressed and He was afflicted, yet He did not open His mouth; like a lamb that is led to slaughter, and like a sheep that is silent before its shearers, so He did not open His mouth.

נגש והוא נענה ולא יפתח-פיו כשה לטבח יובל וכרחל לפני גזזיה נאלמה ולא יפתח פיו:

# He Opened Not His Mouth

**MATTHEW 27:12-14**

And while He was being accused by the chief priests and elders, He made no answer. Then Pilate said to Him, "Do You not hear how many things they testify against You?" And He did not answer him with regard to even a single charge, so that the governor was quite amazed.

## ISAIAH 52:14

As many were astonished at him—his appearance was so marred, beyond human semblance, and his form beyond that of the sons of men. (*RSV*)

כאשר שממו עליך רבים כן-משחת מאיש מראהו ותארו מבני אדם:

## ISAIAH 53:5

But he was wounded for our transgressions, he was bruised for our iniquities; upon him was the chastisement that made us whole and with his stripes we are healed. (*RSV*)

והוא מחלל מפשענו מדכא מעונתינו מוסר שלומנו עליו ובחברתו נרפא-לנו:

**JOHN 19:1-3**

Then Pilate therefore took Jesus, and scourged Him. And the soldiers wove a crown of thorns and put it on His head, and arrayed Him in a purple robe; and they began to come up to Him, and say, "Hail, King of the Jews!" and to give Him blows in the face.

# By His Stripes We Are Healed

# Of Whom Does the Prophet Speak?

For centuries the 53rd chapter of Isaiah has been one of the most pondered prophecies in the Bible. Of whom was the prophet speaking in this magnificent word portrait?

One day a royal official of the country of Ethiopia, a proselyte to the religion of Judaism, was returning home from a pilgrimage to Jerusalem. While he was travelling along, he was reading the 53rd chapter from the scroll of Isaiah and he, also, was trying to ponder its meaning. As he was reading, the Spirit of God led a disciple of Jesus to come up to his chariot. Here's what happened.

"Then Philip ran up to the chariot and heard the man reading Isaiah, the prophet. "Do you understand what you are reading?" Philip asked.

"How can I," he said, "unless someone explains it to me?" So he invited Philip to come up and sit with him.

The Ethiopian eunuch was reading this passage of Scripture: "He was led like a sheep to the slaughter, and as a lamb before the shearer is silent, so he did not open his mouth. In his humiliation he was deprived of justice. Who can speak of his descendants? For his life was taken from the earth" (Isaiah 53:7, 8).

The eunuch asked Philip, "Tell me, please, who is the prophet talking about, himself or someone else?"

The man was obviously a stranger in the land and hadn't heard much about the events surrounding Jesus' life and death, so Philip took the Isaiah scroll and "began with that very passage of Scripture and told him the good news about Jesus" (Acts 8:30-35 NIV).

The reason Philip could preach about Jesus out of Isaiah's writings is because Jesus had so obviously fulfilled Isaiah's predictions about Messiah, and the Ethiopian saw it immediately.

## ISAIAH'S FOUR MESSIANIC CAMEOS

The prophet Isaiah unquestionably had the greatest and the most insights into the life and character of the coming Messiah.

Isaiah's greatest contribution to the profile of Messiah was four prophetic cameos that described vividly the predicted career of one who was called the "Servant of the Lord." These four passages, Isaiah 42:1-9; 49:1-12; 50:4-11 and 52:13—53:12, present a picture of Messiah that increases in clarity and detail until in the last cameo, Isaiah 53, the Servant of the Lord is clearly shown as One who will suffer and die for the sins of Israel but *then* will be highly prospered by the Lord. Although our main interest here is the fourth cameo, Isaiah 53, we'll take a look as we go along at some of the details of this Servant's sufferings which were predicted in the first three cameos.

## THE IDENTITY OF THE SERVANT

For centuries the identity of this Servant has been disputed among Jewish theologians. Some claim that the Servant is Messiah. Others say it refers to Isaiah himself or to the nation of Israel. Some have called this 53rd chapter of Isaiah the "bad conscience of the synagogue" since it's no longer read in most synagogues. Since the description of the Servant in this passage has such a direct relationship to the actual career of Jesus of Nazareth, many Rabbis simply have sought to ignore it altogether.

However, most of the ancient Jewish commentators saw this Servant of the Lord as Messiah. Rabbi Moshe Alshekh, one of the great 17th century expositors from Safed, Israel, said, "Our Rabbis with one voice accept and affirm the opinion that the prophet is speaking of the King Messiah, and we shall ourselves also adhere to the same view." Abarbanel, one of Judaism's greatest 15th century statesmen, philosophers and theologians said, "This is also the opinion of our own learned men in the majority of their Midrashim." The Targum Jonathan, one of the most authoritative Rabbinic sources of the 4th century C.E., interprets much of Isaiah 53 as pertaining to the Messiah and begins the translation, "Behold my servant Messiah."

## COULD THE SERVANT BE "ISRAEL?"

From the 12th century onward a tradition began to develop that the Servant Isaiah spoke of was really the nation of Israel itself, since it had suffered so much and Isaiah's Messiah-Servant was destined to be a suffering one. The thinking was that one generation must suffer for the mistakes of the previous generation.

Now, it is true that the consequences of the sins of ancestors often fall on their descendants. But when this is true, the suffering of the descendants does no good at all for the previous generation who have long since passed off the scene of history. The prediction of the Servant's death in Isaiah's prophecy is completely unique, since it's said to bring real benefit to those whose wickedness he *presently* bears. Obviously then, the Servant can't refer to one righteous generation of Jews suffering for the evils of a previous generation.

Isaiah goes on to say that with the suffering and scourging of the Messiah, there would be healing for men (Isaiah 53:5). It's apparent from the context that Isaiah meant healing from the consequences of the sins of men, since the Servant has their sins laid upon him. The Servant here simply can't be the nation of Israel suffering for the past or future generations of Jews. The death and suffering of this predicted One is said to uniquely make peace and healing possible for the whole nation of Israel, as well as the non-Jews. No amount of persecution that Judaism has suffered has ever brought about this universal healing and peace, and the history of the nature of man is witness to the fact that it never will.

## THE SUFFERINGS OF THE SERVANT

As we've seen already, two pictures of Messiah emerge from the hundreds of prophecies related to him. In some he's the great dynamic ruler who subjects all of God's enemies under his feet and brings about universal peace with all of Israel restored to her land.

The other picture of Messiah, the one who comes to suffer and die for the sins of the people, is the emphasis of Isaiah's portraits of Him. It's predicted that this Servant of the Lord would be treated in such a manner that he would be disfigured to the point that he would hardly look human (Isaiah 52:14). As unthinkable as it is, this Servant would be struck on both the back and face. He would be humiliated by being spit upon in the face (Isaiah 50:4-11).

It's well known that this is the kind of treatment that Jesus received during the six illegal trials he was subjected to. The officers of Herod's temple guard spat in Jesus' face after the Sanhedrin had condemned him. Then they blindfolded him and struck him in the face. A jagged crown of thorns was jammed down on his head and he was cruelly whipped with a Roman scourge. It was a sadistic whip made of many strips of leather to which pieces of bone or jagged metal were attached to make the effect more painful.

None of this abuse of Jesus was either legal or warranted. There had been no criminal charges proven against him. Yet all of this happened to the Servant of the Lord just as Isaiah had prophesied that it would (Isaiah 52:14—52:12).

## THE SOURCE OF HIS SUFFERINGS

If this promised Servant of the Lord was to suffer, at whose hands would this take place and for what reason? In Isaiah's second prophetic cameo we're given the first indication of who will inflict this suffering. He refers to the Servant-Messiah as "the despised one, the one abhorred by the *nation*" (Isaiah 49:7).

It's most unfortunate (and dishonest) that the Revised Standard Version of the Bible and the Jewish Soncino Commentaries translate this passage "... to him who is abhorred by the *nations*." By translating 'nations' plural, it makes it seem as though the Gentiles (who are always referred to as the 'nations') are the ones who despise and abhor the Servant. The idea is fostered here that the Servant is Israel and she is abhorred by the Gentiles. While that may have been true in Jewish history, that particular fact can't be proved by this passage because the word used in the Hebrew text for 'nation' is *goi*, and it is singular and can only honestly be translated as 'nation,' which in this context refers to Israel alone.

Thus, it's predicted by Isaiah that this Servant of the Lord will be despised and abhorred by the nation for whose deliverance he came, Israel.

In his fourth prophetic cameo of Messiah, Isaiah interjects himself with the pronouns "we, us and our" to identify the people for whom this Servant both suffers and is despised by. Since Isaiah was a Hebrew he can be referring to none other than his own nation of Israel. The Servant is always spoken of with the 3rd person singular pronouns, "he, his, him" thus definitely setting him apart from the writer, Isaiah, and his nation Israel.

Any fair analysis of these facts reveals that Isaiah, a Jewish prophet, was identifying his own people as the ones who would despise and reject this Servant of the Lord.

## WHY HATE THE MESSIAH?

The question that must come to mind here is, "Why would they reject and hate their own looked-for Messiah?" The answer lies in the heart of Isaiah 53. Here the prophet scathingly rebukes the waywardness of Israel as far as its relationship to God is concerned. He says, "All of us like sheep have gone astray, each of us has turned to his own way; but the LORD has caused the iniquity [*sin*] of us all to fall on him" (Isaiah 53:6).

Isaiah had previously predicted that a day would come when the people would draw near the LORD with their words and honor him with lipservice, but their hearts would be far from him (Isaiah 29:13).

The people would reject this Suffering Messiah because he would come at a time when their hearts had grown cold to God and indifferent to the fact that they were sinners and that God hates and will judge sin. Naturally they would despise someone whose main message in life was for the people to repent of their spiritual hypocrisy and turn back to God in their hearts, and whose mission in life was to take those 'unadmitted' sins upon himself and suffer the penalty for them which, by the very laws of their sacrificial system, was death.

## WHY MUST MESSIAH SUFFER?

The greatest questions posed in this re-markable prophecy however are, "Why should anyone suffer for the sins of another? What good would it do? Where is it ever taught anywhere in the Scriptures that a man can pay God for another's sins?"

The truth of the matter is, the Hebrew Scriptures teach that each man must pay for his own sinning with the penalty of death, himself. Ezekiel said for God, "The person who sins will die. The son will not bear the punishment for the father's iniquity, nor will the father bear the punishment for the son's iniquity; the righteousness of the righteous will be upon himself, and the wickedness of the wicked will be upon himself" (Ezekiel 18:20).

The Biblical principle was set here; each sinner must die for his own sins. But there was a very special exception inherent in the Mosaic system from its inception. Indeed, it was taught from the beginning of God's dealing with man after he had sinned.

This exception was that God Himself could appoint innocent substitutes to die in the sinner's place, bearing the penalty of death which was really due the sinner. This is why the animal sacrifice system was immediately instituted after the giving of the moral code of the Mosaic Law. Man would surely get around to breaking God's Law, but by faith, he could come to God and offer the appointed animal as a substitute to suffer the judgment of death for his personal sins.

But, it was obvious that the sacrifice of animals couldn't really be a permanent solution for dealing with the problem of man's sins, because the animals had to continually be offered, thus demonstrating that they were not a lasting substitute.

## GOD'S NEW DEAL

In the prophecy of Isaiah 53, we're brought face to face with a whole new concept of atonement for sins. I realize that this is the main source of contention that Judaism has with true Christianity; the idea of Messiah, or any human being, dying as a substitutionary sacrifice for sin. In fact, the main basis on which this passage of Isaiah is rejected as Messianic today is the argument that God would never require a human sacrifice, so therefore this can't literally refer to a person such as they envisioned Messiah to be. It must be symbolic of the nation of Israel suffering and being rejected by men.

There's an important precedent for the concept of a man being offered as a sin-offering, though. Remember that God once asked Abraham to offer his son Isaac as an offering to Him. God of course stopped Abraham from carrying out this command just in the nick-of-time. But, Isaac was spared on the basis of the fact that God would provide another sacrifice in the future that would adequately deal with man's failure to live up to God's laws.

## GOD'S PROVISION ON MT. MORIAH

Abraham understood that his son's life was spared because of this promised provision on the part of God, for he named the mountain, where he had almost sacrificed his only son, "Jehovah-Jireh," which means "The Lord will provide" (Genesis 22:14). That mountain was afterwards called Moriah, the very one on which 2000 years later another "only Son" was crucified. Was the crucified Jesus of Nazareth the one that God had promised to provide as a sin-offering? I think all the evidence bears out the fact that he was.

Isaiah also saw the Servant of the Lord in the role of sin-bearer, for he wrote, "All of us like sheep have gone astray, each of us has turned to his own way; but the Lord has caused the iniquity [*sin*] of us all to fall on him.... By oppression and judgment he was taken away; and as for his generation, who considered that he was cut off [*killed*] out of the land of the living for the transgression of my people to whom the stroke was due?" (53:6, 8). "... He will render himself as a guilt offering" (53:10c). "My Servant will justify the many, as he will bear their iniquities" (53:11d). "He poured out Himself to death ... He himself bore the sin of many" (Isaiah 53:12).

The reason this Servant would qualify to be a substitutionary sin-bearer is also revealed through the Isaiah 53 passage, "He had done no violence, nor was there any deceit in his mouth" (53:9c). He was called "The Righteous One" (53:11c).

The reason is that he himself had no sins for which he could be judged with sin's penalty which is death. Therefore, he alone, of all men, qualified to bear the sins of the guilty and provide a removal of that for which God condemns men, their sins!

The heart of Jesus' teachings is that he came to do just that. He said, "The Son of Man did not come to be served, but to serve, and to give his life a ransom for many" (Mark 10:45). One day he said to his bitter critics, "Which one of you religious leaders can find one tiny sin for which you can convict me? Since you can't, you know I'm speaking the truth, so why don't you believe me?" (paraphrase John 8:46). None of these experts in the Mosaic Law could come up with any real sin to charge him with. Even at his trial the only charge they could agree on was that he claimed to be the Messiah, the Son of God.

## HE OPENED NOT HIS MOUTH

Throughout the trials of Jesus, all present were astonished because he never spoke a word in His own defense. How graphically Isaiah shows Messiah's willing submission to be put to death for the sin of man. Isaiah even cast this prophecy in the imagery of the sacrificial lamb, "He was oppressed and he was afflicted, yet he did not open his mouth; like a lamb that is led to slaughter and like a sheep that is silent before its shearers, so he did not open his mouth" (Isaiah 53:7).

When the officers came to seize Jesus to arrest him, he willingly came out to them. When Peter tried to defend him Jesus stopped him by saying, "All this has taken place that the Scriptures of the prophets may be fulfilled" (Matthew 26:56).

Is the New Testament report of Jesus' fulfilling all of these prophecies of Isaiah's Suffering Servant simply a clever fraud, pieced together by the followers of Jesus long after the events?

It takes more faith to believe that, than I've got! If the religious leaders of Jesus' day could have disproven *any* of his claims of Messiahship, they would have done it gladly and could have discredited this new movement at its beginning. But instead, history records that they put to death those who proclaimed the facts, but they never refuted their arguments.

## PSALM 22:1, 6-8, 14-18

My God, my God, why hast Thou forsaken me? Far from my deliverance are the words of my groaning.

But I am a worm, and not a man, a reproach of men, and despised by the people. All who see me sneer at me; they separate with the lip, they wag the head, saying, "Commit thyself to the Lord; let Him deliver him; let Him rescue him, because He delights in him."

I am poured out like water, and all my bones are out of joint; my heart is like wax; it is melted within me. My strength is dried up like a potsherd, and my tongue cleaves to my jaws; and Thou dost lay me in the dust of death.

For dogs have surrounded me; a band of evildoers has encompassed me; they pierced my hands and my feet. I can count all my bones. They look, they stare at me; they divide my garments among them, and for my clothing they cast lots.

# Messiah's Sufferings

אֵלִי אֵלִי לָמָה עֲזַבְתָּנִי רָחוֹק מִישׁוּעָתִי דִּבְרֵי שַׁאֲגָתִי:

וְאָנֹכִי תוֹלַעַת וְלֹא-אִישׁ חֶרְפַּת אָדָם וּבְזוּי עָם: כָּל-רֹאַי יַלְעִגוּ לִי יַפְטִירוּ בְשָׂפָה יָנִיעוּ

רֹאשׁ: גֹּל אֶל-יְהֹוָה יְפַלְּטֵהוּ יַצִּילֵהוּ כִּי חָפֵץ בּוֹ:

כַּמַּיִם נִשְׁפַּכְתִּי וְהִתְפָּרְדוּ כָּל-עַצְמוֹתָי הָיָה לִבִּי כַּדּוֹנָג נָמֵס בְּתוֹךְ מֵעָי: יָבֵשׁ כַּחֶרֶשׂ

כֹּחִי וּלְשׁוֹנִי מֻדְבָּק מַלְקוֹחָי וְלַעֲפַר-מָוֶת תִּשְׁפְּתֵנִי:

כִּי סְבָבוּנִי כְּלָבִים עֲדַת מְרֵעִים הִקִּיפוּנִי כָּאֲרִי יָדַי וְרַגְלָי: אֲסַפֵּר כָּל-עַצְמוֹתָי הֵמָּה

יַבִּיטוּ יִרְאוּ-בִי: יְחַלְּקוּ בְגָדַי לָהֶם וְעַל-לְבוּשִׁי יַפִּילוּ גוֹרָל:

**PSALM 22:18**

They divide my garments among them, and for
my clothing they cast lots.

יחלקו בגדי להם ועל-לבושי יפילו גורל :

**JOHN 19:23-24**

The soldiers therefore, when they had crucified Jesus, took His outer garments and made four parts, a part to every soldier and also the tunic; now the tunic was seamless, woven in one piece.

They said therefore to one another, "Let us not tear it, but cast lots for it, to decide whose it shall be;" that the Scripture might be fulfilled, "They divided My outer garments among them, and for My clothing they cast lots."

# Casting Lots For His Clothing

Messiah Forsaken

**PSALM 22:1**

My God, my God, why has Thou forsaken me? Far from my deliverance are the words of my groaning.

אלי אלי למה עזבתני רחוק מישועתי דברי שאגתי:

**MATTHEW 27:46**

And about the ninth hour Jesus cried out with a loud voice, saying, "Eli, Eli, lama sabachthani?" that is, "My God, My God, why hast Thou forsaken Me?"

**PSALM 69:21**

They also gave me gall for my food, and for my thirst they gave me vinegar to drink.

ויתנו בברותי ראש ולצמאי ישקוני חמץ:

**PSALM 22:15**

My strength is dried up like a potsherd, and my tongue cleaves to my jaws; and Thou dost lay me in the dust of death.

יבש כחרש כחי ולשוני מדבק מלקוחי ולעפר-מות תשפתני:

**JQHN 19:29**

A jar full of sour wine was standing there; so they put a sponge full of the sour wine upon a branch of hyssop, and brought it up to His mouth.

# Vinegar For His Thirst

# Messiah's Sufferings

Perhaps no other statement that Jesus made has provoked more curiosity and controversy than his cry from the cross, "My God, my God, why have you forsaken me?" (Matthew 27:46).

I don't believe Jesus asked the question because he didn't know the answer. It's that he wanted us to find out what it was and sending us back to David's prophetic Psalm from where it is quoted was a good place to begin.

The Psalms make many predictions concerning the Messiah but the clearest and most graphic of these is Psalm 22. King David wrote this around 1000 B.C.E. yet the circumstances described in this Psalm don't fit anything that ever happened in the life of David himself as so many of his other Psalms do. David ruled the most powerful kingdom of his day and yet never fell into his enemies' hands even during his darkest times, as this Psalm describes of its central figure. David died a peaceful death in old age too, while this personage in Psalm 22 dies in great suffering and humiliation.

## THE SUFFERER OF PSALM 22

Once again, the identity of the one whose sufferings are described in Psalm 22 is of utmost importance. Because of the remarkable features of it which found exact fulfillment in the events of Jesus' crucifixion, his followers have naturally claimed it as a Messianic Psalm. On the other hand, because it does seem so specifically to allude to Jesus, later Rabbis and liberal Christian theologians have either avoided comment on it or sought to ascribe the central personage as someone other than Messiah.

However, in the ancient Rabbinic collection of traditions called the Yalkut, in commenting on Isaiah 60:1, the Rabbis were discussing the sufferings and exaltation of the Messiah. In the section dealing with when the enemies of Messiah will flee from before him, the Rabbis said that God makes an agreement with the Messiah to the effect that the Messiah would suffer for the sins of all Jews who had lived before or after him, and to illustrate these sufferings, they quote

from Psalm 22, "your tongue will cleave to your mouth" and "your strength will be dried up like a potsherd [*broken piece of pottery*]." Three times the Yalkut quotes Psalm 22 as speaking of the sufferings of the Messiah, the Son of David.

## THE VIEW FROM THE CROSS

What we have before us in Psalm 22 is a very personal prophecy of how Messiah *felt* in his sufferings and how he viewed the things going on around him. David, in the power of the Spirit, speaks as if he were the Messiah, feeling his emotions and discouragement as if they were his own.

In one of the most amazing usages of prophecy anywhere in literature, David describes in unbelievably realistic terms the plight of one going through the tortures of crucifixion. Yet, crucifixion was a Phoenecian and Roman custom, unknown to the Jews until approximately 400 years *after* David wrote this Psalm.

It's fairly common knowledge that Jesus was executed on a Roman cross because he claimed to be the Son of God and Israel's Messiah. In fact, above his head on the cross, Pilate whimsically nailed a sign, "Jesus of Nazareth, the King of the Jews." The chief priests tried to get Pilate to change the sign to read, "*He said* he was the King of the Jews" but Pilate wouldn't change it. God was about to unfold the fulfillment of the Messianic sufferings of Psalm 22 and He wanted the whole world to know that it was happening to His chosen Messiah, Jesus of Nazareth.

Listen to the description of the actual sufferings which happened to Jesus on the cross, 1000 years after the Psalmist described it:

"*I am poured out like water....*" This describes Jesus' heavy perspiration as he suffered in the intense Middle-Eastern sun.

"*All my bones are out of joint....*" This is one of the most excruciating results of hanging suspended by outstretched arms. The muscles fatigue and stretch. The bones are pulled out of joint by the person's own weight.

"*My heart is like wax, it is melted into my*

*bowels....*" Many feel that Jesus' heart ruptured from the stress and the pericardial sack surrounding the heart filled with blood.

"*My strength is dried up like a fragment of pottery, and my tongue cleaves to my jaws....*" This describes the horrible thirst from dehydration and lack of water in the scorching sun. In Psalm 69:21 this thirst is specifically predicted, "... for my thirst they gave me vinegar to drink."

The Apostle John in the New Testament records the fulfillment of this prophecy:

"Later, knowing that all was now completed, and so that the Scripture would be fulfilled, Jesus said, 'I am thirsty.' A jar of wine vinegar was there, so they soaked a sponge in it, put the sponge on a stalk of the hyssop plant and lifted it to Jesus' lips. When he had received the drink, Jesus said, 'It is finished.' With that he bowed his head and gave up his life" (John 19:28-30).

## "THEY PIERCED MY HANDS AND FEET"

Nothing in the ancient Jewish means of punishment involved the piercing of hands and feet. The Jews' main means of execution was stoning. And yet, here is the Messiah, saying through David's pen, that one day his hands and feet would be pierced.

Obviously, the meaning of this phrase is vigorously contested by the Rabbis since to admit that it means exactly what it says is tantamount to admitting that Jesus, whom they had crucified, was their Messiah.

The main objection to this phrase revolves around one word, "to pierce." In the Hebrew Massoretic text, the Hebrew word is "caari" which translates into "like a lion." Thus the Jewish Bible reads, "Like a lion they are at my hands and my feet." However, the 3rd century B.C.E. translation of the Hebrew Old Testament into Greek (the Septuagint), designated this disputed word as "caaru" which means "to pierce." Thus, 250 years before Jesus' crucifixion would have made anyone prejudiced about this reading, the Rabbis were translating the word as "pierced." The only minute difference in these two words is the length of the stem of the last letter of the Hebrew word, and it could easily have been altered by one tiny slip on one stroke of a scribe's pen.

## WHY WAS HE PIERCED AND FORSAKEN?

The penetrating question that begins Psalm 22 is the same cry which Jesus screamed from the cross as darkness fell across the whole land at mid-day, "My God, my God, why have you forsaken me?" Never were such words of utter aloneness expressed by human lips! Never in human history was there so much at stake and so few who cared about it.

Jesus had gone through horrible physical torture up to this point without a whimper of pain. Yet at this point, the dreaded "cup" which he had asked God to remove from him, if possible, now had to be drunk to its last dreg. As God's appointed sacrificial substitute for man, he hung there on the cross and allowed Jehovah God to put on him the sins of every man and woman who would ever live. He was then judged with their guilt and had to suffer sin's penalty which is death and separation from God (see Isaiah 59:1, 2). For a sinless one like Jesus who had never known a moment's separation from fellowship with his holy Father, the mental anguish of being forsaken by Him was more than his human emotions could bear and thus his scream.

## GAMBLING FOR HIS GARMENT

In some ways, the most unusual prediction in Psalm 22 is this, "They divide my garments among them and for my clothing they cast lots" (verse 18). This seemingly insignificant detail was thrown in by the Psalmist at the instruction of the Spirit of God. Little did the Roman soldiers know the drama they were engulfed in when they decided to gamble for Jesus' garment. They were no students of Jewish prophecy and yet as they knelt there, indifferently shooting dice at the foot of the cross in fulfillment of prophecy, above them on the cross, the eternal destiny of mankind was being settled (John 19:23, 24).

I'm reminded here of the question posed by the writer of the Epistle to the Hebrews so long ago, "What make us think that we can escape if we are indifferent to this great salvation announced by the Lord Jesus himself, and passed on to us by those who heard him speak?" (Hebrews 2:3 TLB).

**JOEL 2:30-31**

"And I will display wonders in the sky and on the earth, blood, fire, and columns of smoke. The sun will be turned into darkness, and the moon into blood, before the great and awesome day of the Lord comes."

ונתתי־מופתים בשמים ובארץ דם ואש ותימרות עשן : השמש יהפך לחשך והירח
לדם לפני בוא יום יהוה הגדול :

# Upheaval of Nature

**MATTHEW 27:45, 50, 51**

Now from the sixth hour darkness fell upon all the land until the ninth hour. And Jesus cried out again with a loud voice, and yielded up His spirit. And behold, the veil of the temple was torn in two from top to bottom, and the earth shook; and the rocks were split.

**NUMBERS 9:12**

They shall leave none of it until morning, nor break a bone of it; according to all the statute of the Passover they shall observe it.

לא־ישאירו ממנו עד־בקר ועצם לא ישברו־בו ככל־חקת הפסח יעשו אתו:

**JOHN 19:32, 33, 36**

The soldiers therefore came, and broke the legs of the first man, and of the other man who was crucified with Him; but coming to Jesus, when they saw that He was already dead, they did not break His legs; for these things came to pass, that the Scripture might be fulfilled. "Not a bone of Him shall be broken."

# Not a Bone Broken

# He Was Pierced

**ZECHARIAH 12:10**

And I will pour out on the house of David and on the inhabitants of Jerusalem the Spirit of grace and of supplication, so that they will look on Me whom they have pierced; and they will mourn for Him, as one mourns for an only son, and they will weep bitterly over Him, like the bitter weeping over Him.

ושפכתי על-בית דויד ועל יושב ירושלם רוח חן ותחנונים והביטו אלי את אשר-
דקרו וספדו עליו כמספד על-היחיד והמר עליו כהמר על-הבכור :

**JOHN 19:34, 37**

But one of the soldiers pierced His side with a spear, and immediately there came out blood and water. And again another Scripture says, "They shall look on Him whom they pierced."

# Upheaval of Nature

A popular book of a few years ago was called *The Passover Plot* by Hugh Schonfield. The basic premise of the book is that Jesus had a Messiah complex and he and his disciples deliberately plotted to fulfill the Old Testament prophecies about Messiah.

There are certain things that a man can have no control over and we've looked at a number of prophecies already that no one could have staged. This last series of three pictures fall into that category as we'll see now.

In a backhanded way, Schonfield's book does a service to those who believe in Jesus as Messiah for he admits that there are two things that are definitely historical facts. First, Jesus of Nazareth did live and die on this earth and in so doing fulfilled certain Messianic prophecies.

Secondly, he acknowledges that there were certain prophecies which were generally recognized as Messianic before and during the era of Jesus' life. This point is proven by the fact that "456 Old Testament prophecies are applied to Messiah by the most ancient Jewish writings," according to Dr. Edersheim who lists them all with their references. He also shows that these are supported by more than 558 separate quotations from Rabbinic writings.[1]

Where Schonfield runs into trouble is in trying to explain certain phenomena associated with the Messianic prophecies over which Jesus obviously had no control. One of those situations is the following:

## UPHEAVAL OF NATURE
### (Joel 2:30, 31)

Many Old Testament prophecies speak of peculiar upheavals of nature and terrifying astrological signs preceding the setting up of the days of Messiah. None of these prophecies will be completely fulfilled until the actual coming of Messiah with power

---

[1]Edersheim, *Life and Times of Jesus*, Appendix IX

and glory to set up the Kingdom of God and judge His enemies.

A principle that's absolutely necessary to understand in interpreting prophecy is a law called "The law of double fulfillment." Simply stated, this involves any two or more predicted events widely separated in time as far as their fulfillment is concerned, but they are brought together within the scope of one prophecy. The first, *partial* fulfillment, becomes a further assurance of the second, more complete fulfillment.

## NATURE REACTS TO CRUCIFIXION

This principle is illustrated in the case of the prophecy of Joel 2:28-32. Some of the natural catastrophes predicted occurred during the crisis events of Jesus' last hours on earth.

In his sermon on the day of Pentecost, Peter quoted Joel's prophecy of the upheaval of nature which was to take place at Messiah's coming and pointed out that the fact that the sun turned into darkness when Jesus was crucified was a partial fulfillment of that prophecy (Acts 2:14-39). In a reference to this same predicted cataclysm in nature which would herald Messiah's appearance, Matthew records, "When Jesus had cried out again in a loud voice, he gave up his spirit. At that moment the curtain of the Temple was torn in two from the top to bottom. The earth shook and the rocks split" (Matthew 27:50, 51 NIV).

As awesome as those occurrences were, the greater fulfillment of this passage, as indicated by the context, will be at the coming of Messiah to set up the long postponed Kingdom of God.

## NOT A BONE BROKEN
### (Numbers 9:12; John 19:32, 33, 36)

This prophecy is wrapped up in the fact that the sacrificial Passover lamb was a *type* of Messiah giving himself as a sacrifice which would cause God to "pass-over" man in judgment. Just as God spared each family who took the blood of the lamb their last night in Egypt and applied it to their doorpost so that God would pass over their house with his Death Angel, so God says He will spare His wrathful judgment to all those who symbolically apply to their hearts the blood of His great and final Passover Lamb, Messiah-Jesus.

Jesus was called "The Lamb of God" and it was for this role as a substitute sacrificial lamb that he came into this world. However, since God had prescribed specific instructions about what this Passover Lamb must be like and what must happen to it, if Jesus was going to fulfill this symbol in type, the same things would have to happen to him. He would have to be *without blemish*, that is, without sin (Exodus 12:5). He would need to be *eaten*. This was how Jesus illustrated the act of believing in him in John 6:47-58. He compared it to *eating his flesh and drinking his blood*. In other words, taking him inside of them and making him a part of their very being. He would also have to be *sacrificed on the exact day of Passover* and it's well known that Jesus was killed on that day.

Another important feature about the prescribed Passover Lamb was that *not a bone of his body could be broken* (Exodus 12:46). When Jesus had already died, the religious leaders, not aware of his death, petitioned Pilate to break the legs of Jesus and the two criminals in order to speed up their death so they could be taken down from the cross before the special Sabbath which followed Passover.

So Pilate sent soldiers to break the legs of all three men. The soldiers broke the legs of the two criminals but when they came to Jesus and found him already dead, they didn't break his legs, and in disobeying this specific order, they unwittingly fulfilled the prophecy that "none of the Passover Lamb's bones should be broken" (see John 19:31-33).

## HE WAS PIERCED
(Zechariah 12:10)

Picture if you will the two Roman soldiers standing before Jesus, somewhat amazed that He's already dead. There's no need to break his legs now. But, just on a whim one of them decides to thrust his long spear up into Jesus' side, and with deadly accuracy it goes right through his heart. The fact that blood and water gushed out, showing that the clear-looking serum had already begun to separate from the blood cells, confirmed that he was dead (John 19:34).

Only a whim on the soldier's part, but it fulfilled a prophecy made unerringly five centuries before by the prophet Zechariah:

"And I will pour out on the House of David and on the inhabitants of Jerusalem the Spirit of grace and supplication so that they will look on me *whom they pierced;* and they will mourn for him as one mourns for an only son, and they will weep bitterly over him, like the bitter weeping over a first-born" (Zechariah 12:10).

In the whole twelfth chapter of Zechariah, he predicts a time when the remnant of Israel will be in desperate peril and Messiah returns to earth to save them from certain destruction by the warring nations of the world who are massed all around Israel. It's at the moment that the believing remnant of Israel sees that the one delivering them is the same one whom they caused to be pierced 2000 years ago, that the ultimate fulfillment of this prophecy will take place.

There are three key points that unlock Zechariah's prophecy in chapter twelve. *First,* the God of Israel would at some time in their history be pierced at the instigation of Israel. *Secondly,* this piercing which is expressly charged to "the House of David and the inhabitants of Jerusalem" has to have happened *before* Messiah comes in power and glory to rescue and establish believing Israel in her Kingdom, for after that he'll be reigning forever and no such piercing will be possible. This leads one to conclude that King-Messiah must have been on earth at some time in another role and was pierced and suffered at that time.

*Thirdly,* the response of the Jews at seeing that their King-Messiah is none other than the rejected Jesus of Nazareth will be one of uncontrollable sorrow and repentance. The prophet John said that when Jesus returns to earth "every eye will see him, even those who pierced him, and all the tribes of the earth will mourn over him" (Rev. 1:7).

# The Lamb of God

**PSALM 40:6-8**

"Sacrifice and offering you have not desired, but a body you have prepared for me; in whole burnt offering and sacrifices for sin you have taken no pleasure. Then I said, 'Behold, I have come to do your will, O God (in the roll of the book it is written of me).'" (LXX)

זבח ומנחה לא חפצת אזנים כרית לי
עולה וחטאה לא שאלת: אז אמרתי
הנה-באתי במגלת-ספר כתוב עלי: לע-
שות-רצונך אלהי חפצתי ותורתך בתוך
מעי:

**HEBREWS 10:10-14**

By this will we have been sanctified through the offering of the body of Jesus Christ once for all. And every priest stands daily ministering and offering time after time the same sacrifices, which can never take away sins; but He, having offered one sacrifice for sins for all time, sat down at the right hand of God, waiting from that time onward until His enemies be made a footstool for His feet. For by one offering He has perfected for all time those who are sanctified.

# The Lamb of God

In this chapter you're going to have to put on your thinking-cap because the arguments and logic these Old and New Testament scholars use to present Messiah as a *divine* person who clothed himself with a human body at a point in history, is so close and so intriguing that you won't want to miss a single nuance of their meaning.

## GOD BECOMES 'FLESH'

To many devout worshippers of Jehovah God, it's the quintessence of blasphemy to say that there was a time when He took on a human body and lived on earth in that manner for any length of time. And yet, there are specific predictions in the Old Testament that that very thing would happen when Messiah came to earth.

Psalm 40 is one of the prophetic passages which alludes to this when it says that God had no real pleasure in burnt offerings and sacrifices even though they were His divinely ordained way of handling sin and its consequences during Old Testament times. The Psalmist predicted that there would come a time when God would no longer require sacrifice. It would be at a time when God prepared a body for the Promised One who was going to come and do God's will on earth. We've seen from many prophecies already that this Coming One was none other than the divine Messiah of Israel.

A very ancient Jewish interpretation in the Midrash concerning Messiah's geneology makes reference to Psalm 40 and says that this is definitely Messiah speaking through the Psalmist. The New Testament writer of the epistle to the Hebrews quotes Psalm 40:6-8 from the Greek Septuagint version and uses it as the basis for his climactic argument to convince the Hebrew followers of Jesus that his sacrificial death *fulfilled* and thus *annuled* the Mosaic animal sacrifice system.

## NO MORE SACRIFICE NEEDED

It's impossible for us today to realize the full impact of a statement like that on people whose whole lives revolved around the system of animal sacrifices and the temporary forgiveness of sins which it procured. In order for them to believe the truth that no more animal sacrifices needed to be offered, the writer of Hebrews had to present *very* convincing proofs to them from their own scriptures that this was so.

One of the key arguments he uses is the prophetic Psalm 40 which centers on the fact that God had prepared a body for this One who was to come to do His will. As might be expected, there's quite a present day dispute about the phrase in Psalm 40 "... a body you prepared for me." In the official Hebrew Massoretic text it reads instead, "My ears you have opened." However, the Septuagint version of the Old Testament (250 B.C.E.) translates this phrase as "but a body you prepared for me."

The best evidence available indicates that both of these translations are very ancient and genuine. So, why the difference?

The best explanation is that the Septuagint translators of the Hebrew Old Testament, writing sometime before 200 B.C.E. paraphrased the meaning of this portion of Psalm 40. This paraphrasing is known as *targumming* and it was a standard practice in the translating of the Biblical writings. Paraphrasing didn't deny the meaning of the original words, it usually put it into an idiom or concept which was more familiar to the people of their day.

This is the case with the phrase "to open or pierce a person's ears." It was related to completely and voluntarily submitting one's self to another. The idea is beautifully expressed in Exodus 21:2-6 where the case of a slave who loves his master and volunteers to be a lifetime slave to him is discussed. Moses instructs the master to pierce the slave's ear with an awl and that will be a sign that he's volunteered to serve him for his lifetime.

So, the opening or piercing of the ear was a sign and symbol of voluntarily presenting yourself as a slave forever. This idea was interpreted and paraphrased in the Septuagint by the Hebrew scholars as "a body you have prepared for me," because this was a corresponding Greek idea of total submission which the Greek speaking readers of the Septuagint translation would be more familiar with.

## THE SACRIFICE THAT SATISFIED

If the Messiah was to come and dwell in a special body which God had prepared for him, what would be the purpose of it?

There are many facets to the answer of that question, but primarily it was so that, as a sinless man, God could place on him the sins of all mankind and then the body of this special man, which God counted as a fulfillment of the sacrificial lamb, could suffer sin's penalty which is death and God could accept this death as substitutionary for every man who would ever place faith in its efficacy for him.

That's what Isaiah had in mind when he predicted that "God would lay on him [*Messiah*] the sins of us all" (Isaiah 53:6). It's also the heart of what all the New Testament writers taught about Jesus' role as "The Lamb of God." Peter wrote, "… knowing that you were not redeemed with perishable things like silver or gold … but with the precious blood as of a lamb unblemished and spotless, the blood of Christ. For He was foreknown before the foundation of the world but has appeared in these last times for the sake of you … " (1 Peter 1:18-20).

## SACRIFICES INHERENT IN JUDAISM

The concept of sacrificial substitute for sins was inherent in ancient Judaism, although it isn't predominant in Judaism today. But even ancient Rabbinic expositors could understand Psalm 40's message that burnt offerings and animal sacrifices were not God's desired or ultimate plan for dealing with man's sin.

The writer of the book of Hebrews, a man thoroughly immersed in all of Judaism's teachings, really summed up the inadequacy of the animal sacrifices of the Mosaic Law:

"The Law [*of Moses*] is only a shadow of the good things that were to come—not the realities themselves. For this reason it can never, by the same sacrifices repeated endlessly year after year, make perfect those who draw near to worship. If it could, wouldn't they have stopped being offered? For the worshippers would have been cleansed once for all, and would no longer have felt guilty for their sins. But those sacrifices are an annual reminder of sins, because it is impossible for the blood of bulls and goats to take away sins" (Hebrews 10:1-4 NIV).

The logic here is irrefutable. If the animal sacrifices really took sin away, there would have been no need for continual sacrifice. But because of the continual reminder that their sins were only temporarily covered by the animal sacrifices, there was a need for a sacrifice that wouldn't just cover sin, but would take it away forever as a barrier between man and God.

## THE 'GOOD THINGS' TO COME

When the writer of Hebrews said that the Law was only a shadow of the "good things to come" and not their reality, what he had in mind was the *permanent* solution God had planned in bringing his Messiah-Lamb into the world and once and for all judging sin in his substitutionary sacrifice. God's plan was to do away with the whole system of sacrifice and daily appeasement of His wrath and in so doing fulfill the *need* for the external, ritualistic Mosaic Law.

Since God's Messiah, Jesus, has accomplished this role as sin-bearer, God is now free to forgive men's sins purely on the basis of their faith in that *permanent* sacrifice. He can now write his laws in men's hearts and come and live within them in the person of His Holy Spirit and empower men to keep his laws out of a motive of love and gratitude.

Jesus, the Messiah, was the "good thing" who came. As the Psalmist said of him, "O taste and see that the Lord is good" (Psalm 34:8).

## ISAIAH 53:9

His grave was assigned to be with wicked men, yet with a rich man in His death; although He had done no violence, nor was there any deceit in His mouth.

ויתן את־רשעים קברו ואת־עשיר במתיו על לא־חמס עשה ולא מרמה בפיו :

## MATTHEW 27:57-60

And when it was evening, there came a rich man from Arimathea, named Joseph, who himself had also become a disciple of Jesus. This man came to Pilate and asked for the body of Jesus. Then Pilate ordered it to be given over to him.

And Joseph took the body and wrapped it in a clean linen cloth, and laid it in his own new tomb, which he had hewn out in the rock; and he rolled a large stone against the entrance of the tomb and went away.

# Buried By a Rich Man

# Buried By a Rich Man

God always has a way of getting the last word! In the matter of the burial of Jesus this was really the case.

In Isaiah's prophecy concerning Messiah's death, he wrote, "His grave was assigned to be with wicked men, yet he was with a rich man in his death; because he had done no violence, neither was there any deceit in his mouth" (Isaiah 53:9 literal translation).

Only divine foreknowledge could have caused Isaiah to write such a seemingly insignificant thing and only Divine Providence could have worked out all the intricate circumstances necessary to make it happen just the way Isaiah predicted.

Isaiah had forecast in 700 B.C.E. that when the Messiah came to his people, he would die. Nothing could have been further from the expectation of the Jews of Isaiah's time. But Isaiah faithfully recorded his prophecies of this death. He showed that the Messiah's executors would intend to bury him in company with criminals but, contrary to what would be the subseqnent normal burial, Isaiah predicted that he would be buried in connection with a rich man.

In the popular thinking of Isaiah's day a man's burial ought to be fitting to the character and position of his life. Criminals and evil men should receive a poor burial, perhaps even in severe cases the body would just be thrown out in a field to rot or be eaten by wild animals. A good man, however, should have a first rate tomb and a well attended funeral.

Isaiah said that the Messiah's executors intended him to be buried with evil men, since that's exactly what they would consider him. However, he added, their plans wouldn't come off as expected because the Messiah would actually be associated with a rich man in his death since in reality he wasn't evil and had committed no crime.

## THE BURIAL OF JESUS

The executors of Jesus of Nazareth, the Sanhedrin and the Roman governor Pontius Pilate, had assigned Jesus to be crucified with two common criminals. Naturally they assumed that he should be buried as a criminal too and perhaps under ordinary circumstances Jesus would have been. But God had other plans for his Suffering-Messiah.

It was no ordinary day on which the Lamb of God was being crucified. This was the day of preparation for the Passover, the biggest and most awesome feast day of the year. The Sanhedrin had had to hurry to obtain Jesus' conviction and execution before the Passover started. Now, little time remained until sundown of their Passover Sabbath.

So, since these religious leaders were so busy 'doing their religious thing,' and since they assumed that the Roman soldiers would attend to the dirty work of disposing of the body of Jesus with the other criminals, they were content to let things take their own course in this matter.

## BURIED WITH A RICH MAN

But what these leaders hadn't reckoned on was that one of their most respected members of the Sanhedrin, a rich and powerful man named Joseph of Arimathea, would see to it that Jesus got the kind of burial that befit his character and life. The Apostle John describes this unexpected development, "And after these things, Joseph of Arimathea, being a disciple of Jesus, but a secret one, for fear of the Jews, asked Pilate that he might take away the body of Jesus; and Pilate granted permission. He came therefore, and took away his body. And Nicodemus came also, who had first come to Jesus by night ..." (John 19:38, 39a).

Suddenly the 'secret-service believer,' Joseph, cast aside his cloak of fear and marched into Pilate's private audience room to request the body of Jesus for burial. Frankly, Pilate had personally had his fill of the whole mess. Perhaps knowing that according to Jewish custom no body could be left unburied during the night, once he determined that Jesus was dead, he allowed

Joseph to bury the body.

Nicodemus, another Sanhedrin member, and one considered to be the leading teacher of Judaism at that time, also stepped forward to declare his faith in *this* teacher as Messiah. Both of these influen-tial men knew that to be associated with Jesus' burial would be viewed by the rest of the Sanhedrin as agreeing with what Jesus had taught. But the shock of Jesus' violent death and certainly their awareness of his having fulfilled so many Messianic prophecies, caused these two men to publicly identify themselves with Jesus.

As these two newly discovered brothers took the body of Jesus and knelt to prepare it for burial in Joseph's private tomb, they were perhaps too numb with their loss to realize that they were fitting into the fulfillment of Isaiah's prophecy made 700 years before, "He was buried with a rich man in his death" (Isaiah 53:9).

## THE BURIAL 'EVIDENCES'

Unknowingly these men helped to set the stage in such a way that there would be irrefutable circumstantial evidences for the bodily resurrection of Jesus three days later. Nicodemus had brought about 100 pounds of burial spices called myrrh and aloes. These items cost about the equivalent of a common man's wages for one year.

It's important to note certain things about the nature of these two spices. According to the Greek language authorities, Arndt and Gingrich, myrrh was a resinous gum-like material with a strong spicy smell. Aloes was an aromatic quick-drying sap of a tree. These two spices were mixed together and used to coat the strips of linen which were one to two inches wide. These bandages, coated with the shellac-like spices, were then carefully wrapped around each limb of Jesus' dead body according to the Jewish burial custom. Once the aloes dried, the linen wrappings became like a molded cocoon around the body.

After this preparation, they sealed Jesus in Joseph's hewn-out rock tomb by rolling a large stone into a prepared groove cut in the stone in front of the opening (Matthew 27:60). Scholars estimate that a slab large enough to cover the standard entrance of about three feet by five feet would weigh approximately one ton.

## THE PANIC BACK AT THE TEMPLE

In the meantime, one of the religious leaders who had been busily preparing his body and soul for the celebration of Passover, suddenly remembered Jesus' prediction that he would be bodily raised from the dead on the third day. Hurrying to Pilate, he and his fellow Sanhedrinists pressured him into assigning a maximum security guard of Roman soldiers around Jesus' tomb to prevent a 'fake' resurrection by the disciples. Matthew describes this scene, " 'Sir,' they said, 'we remember that while he was still alive that imposter said, "After three days I will rise again." So give the order for the tomb to be made secure until the third day. Otherwise, his disciples may come and steal the body and tell people that he has risen from the dead. Then this last deception will be worse than the first.'

'Take a guard,' Pilate answered. 'Go, make the tomb as secure as you know how.' So they went and made the tomb secure by putting a seal on the stone and posting the guard" (Matthew 27:63-66 NIV).

The seal was a small strand of string stretched from the stone slab to the wall of the outside of the tomb. It was affixed by two dabs of wax with the seal of Rome on it. To open the tomb by moving the stone and breaking the string would be to defy the power and authority of Rome and everyone knew that meant death.

The guards posted at the tomb were tough legionnaires of Rome. In cases like this, a minimum of four soldiers would be on duty. Vegetius, the author of the ancient, "Military Institutes of the Romans," says that the penalty for sleeping on watch was death. So strictest attention to duty was always observed.

In spite of all these elaborate precautions taken by desperate men, three days later the tomb of Jesus was empty. They did their best to keep his body in the tomb but in so doing they overstepped themselves and provided the conditions for the greatest possible evidence to prove that Jesus was resurrected bodily from the dead three days later, just as he said he would be.

**PSALM 16:9-10**

Therefore my heart is glad and my glory rejoices; my flesh also shall rest in hope. For thou wilt not leave my soul in hell neither wilt thou suffer thine Holy One to see corruption. (*KJV*)

לכן שמח לבי ויגל כבודי אף-בשרי ישכן לבטח: כי לא-תעזב נפשי לשאול לא-
תתן חסידך לראות שחת:

He Is Risen

**PSALM 21:4**

He asked life of Thee, Thou didst give it to him, length of days forever and ever.

חיים שאל ממך נתתה לו ארך ימים עולם ועד :

# He Is Risen

A fact often overlooked and seldom emphasized is that the first 100,000 or more of the most ardent disciples of Jesus were all Jews who had been trained in Judaism, were familiar with the Rabbinic teachings about the Messianic prophecies, and for the most part were on the scenes of the public life and death of Jesus. In their minds, they hadn't 'converted' to another religion in order to believe in Jesus and his teachings. They saw in him the One that all of Judaism had been looking for for centuries and it was the most natural thing in the world to embrace him as their long-awaited Messiah.

The life and teachings of Jesus, as well as the controversy surrounding him, had put the small country of Israel into an uproar. After all, you can't minister in such a small area for more than three years, leaving a trail of miraculous healings and antagonizing a powerful minority of critics without becoming the topic of conversation everywhere. Jesus had taught so many new things about God, and man's relationship to him, that it had reached into the very souls of the listeners with transforming power, in spite of the preconditioning of traditions that were often at variance with him.

The relentless opposition against Jesus by the small band of religious leaders had forced the common people to become involved with the controversial question, "Is this prophet from Galilee false or is he the Messiah as he claims?"

## THE 'UNEXPECTED' EMPTY TOMB

After the hubbub of Jesus' many trials and then the public execution of this controversial figure, the curiosity about this whole situation didn't subside as the Rabbis had hoped. I'm sure the Sanhedrin simply decided the best strategy for them was to just bide their time and wait it out and the public interest and curiosity about Jesus would die out in time.

But no one in the city was prepared for the electrifying events of the third day after Jesus' death. As some of the women went to the tomb, an angel of the Lord appeared and told them that Jesus was not there. He had risen just as he said. The angel instructed them to return to Jesus' disciples and tell them the news.

By this time, the Roman soldiers had already discovered that the tomb was empty and had run into the city and reported it to the chief priests. The news began to spread throughout the crowded throngs like wildfire. The religious leaders were desperately trying to explain the situation by blaming the disciples for stealing the body. The Roman soldiers were terrified at the possibility that they might be executed for failing their duty. Even the disciples of Jesus were bewildered and uncertain about what it all meant.

## HE SAID HE WAS GOING TO DO IT!

One thing that none of these people could get out of their minds, however, was the gnawing remembrance that Jesus had predicted that he would be raised from the dead on the third day (Mark 8:31).

No doubt thousands crowded to the small garden of Joseph of Arimathea to look for themselves at his empty tomb. Rumors had begun to circulate about what had happened to Jesus' body. Because it had been so closely guarded, it was hard to believe that anyone could have gotten in to steal it.

Piece by piece the story of the first eyewitnesses began to leak out. There was talk of the strange condition of the burial wrappings which had been on Jesus' body. They had been found intact in the exact shape of his body, yet he wasn't in it. It was like a cocoon. The aloes had hardened and it was impossible to remove Jesus' body and leave the grave clothes in the condition they were found. John, one of the disciples of Jesus, as he looked into the tomb, had actually come to the conclusion that Jesus had miraculously been raised from the dead just on the basis of this evidence alone (John 20:1-9).

Jesus met with his disciples and assured them that he was really alive from the dead. But the reality of everything that had taken place didn't fully hit them until 50 days later when a strange phenomenon occurred in Jerusalem. One hundred and twenty of Jesus' disciples who had been gathered together for prayer, received the special indwelling of the Spirit of God which Jesus had promised would be given to them after he returned to the Father.

Filled with an almost uncontrollable love and boldness, they burst out into the streets speaking about the mighty works of God and proclaiming praises to him. As a great crowd gathered, one of the followers of Jesus, named Peter (the one who had denied even knowing Jesus on the day of his crucifixion) spoke out as boldly as a lion and gave a powerful explanation of the death and strange disappearance of Jesus' body. In rapid fire he threw out prophecy after prophecy which had been fulfilled by the events of Jesus' life and death. No one in the crowd could refute what he said because they had all heard these same prophecies applied to Messiah many times in their synagogues. As Peter spoke, thousands became convinced that Jesus was the Promised Messiah.

## RESURRECTION FORETOLD

Let's listen to a part of this convincing sermon, just as it came from Peter's mouth:

"Men of Israel, listen to this: Jesus of Nazareth was a man accredited by God to you by miracles, wonders and signs, which God did among you through him, as you yourselves know. This man was handed over to you by God's set purpose and foreknowledge; and you, with the help of wicked men, put him to death by nailing him to the cross. But God raised him from the dead, freeing him from the agony of death, because it was impossible for death to keep its hold on him. David said about him: '... my body also will live in hope, because you will not abandon me to the grave, nor will you let your Holy One undergo decay . . .' " (Psalm 16:9, 10).

"Brothers, I can tell you confidently that the patriarch David died and was buried, and his tomb is here to this day [so therefore he couldn't have been talking about himself]. But he was a prophet and knew that God had promised with an oath that he would place one of his descendants on his throne. See-

ing what was ahead, he spoke of the resurrection of the Christ [Messiah], that he was not abandoned to the grave, nor did his body undergo decay. God has raised this Jesus to life, and we are all witnesses of the fact. Exalted to the right hand of God, he has received from the Father the promised Holy Spirit, and has poured out what you now see and hear.... Therefore, let all Israel be assured of this: God has made this Jesus whom you crucified both Lord and Christ [Messiah]" (portions of Acts 2:22-36 with author's clarifications, NIV).

## PROOFS OF THE RESURRECTION

From these few evidences that we've examined, plus the many more which space doesn't permit, certain things about Jesus' resurrection become obvious. *First*, all who had heard him were aware that he had staked his whole credibility on the tenuous prediction that he would come back bodily alive on the third day after death.

*Secondly*, in spite of every precaution taken by the authorities, Jesus' body was missing from the tomb on the third day and there has never been a credible explanation given for that fact except the resurrection. Simon Greenleaf, former head of the Harvard Law School, said that the resurrection of Jesus was one of the best attested facts in history.

*Thirdly*, all the facts of Jesus' death and resurrection perfectly agreed with the pattern predicted in the prophets. *Fourthly*, more than 500 Jewish people testified that on one occasion when they'd all been together, they saw him alive. All eleven of his closest disciples testified that they'd eaten with him after the resurrection. Most of these died martyr's deaths rather than renounce their testimony.

*Fifthly*, there was a radical change which came over the followers of Jesus after they'd seen him and even more so after he went back to the Father and sent the Holy Spirit to reside in them.

*Finally*, within the first year thousands of God-fearing Jewish people believed in Jesus as Messiah, including many of the religious hierarchy (Acts 2:41; 4:1-4; 6:7).

All of this happened because Jesus rose from the dead!

The Ascension

## PSALM 110:1-2

The Lord says to my Lord: "Sit at My right hand, until I make Thine enemies a footstool for Thy feet." The Lord will stretch forth Thy strong scepter from Zion, saying, "Rule in the midst of Thine enemies."

נאם יהוה לאדני שב לימיני עד-אשית איביך הדם לרגליך :  מטה-עזך ישלח יהוה
מציון רדה בקרב איביך :

## MATTHEW 28:18

And Jesus came up and spoke to them, saying, "All authority has been given to Me in heaven and on earth."

## ACTS 1:9

And after He had said these things, He was lifted up while they were looking on, and a cloud received Him out of their sight.

# The Ascension

The remarkable prophecy of Psalm 110 was written by King David about 1000 B.C.E.. Even though some modern scholarship has discounted it as being Messianic, nearly all the Biblical scholars prior to Jesus' time recognized this Psalm as referring to Messiah. This is evident from the mention of it in the Midrash as well as a conversation Jesus had with some Pharisees of his day. These religious leaders of Israel were contending with him about his claim of being Messiah so he put a question to them, "What do you think about the Christ [*Messiah*]. Whose Son is He?"

Without batting an eye they replied matter-of-factly, "The Son of David." There was no debate on that issue. It was clearly understood that when Messiah came he would be that Greater Son of David which the prophet Nathan had predicted would rule over the Kingdom of God forever (1 Chronicles 17:11-14).

Admitting that Messiah would be the Son of David, however, was not tantamount to claiming that he would be divine or equal with God, even though they knew he was to reign forever from David's throne. There were some of their past Rabbis who had taught that Messiah would be divine, but others felt that he would only be a great human being with extraordinary wisdom and power.

## JESUS MAKES THEM FACE THE ISSUE!

Once Jesus got the Pharisees to agree with him that Messiah would be David's son, then he put this question to them: "How then does David in the Spirit call this 'son' of his, Lord?," and then he quoted David in Psalm 110:1, "The LORD [Jehovah] said to *my Lord*, 'Sit at my right hand, until I put your enemies under your feet.' "

"If David calls this person who is to sit at the LORD'S right hand, 'my Lord,' " Jesus asked, "How can he then be his son?" They fully realized that what he was saying to them was that this 'son' of David was more than just a man if David himself called him 'his Lord,' and since they had no comeback, they walked away in silence.

## LEFT WITHOUT ANSWERS

What was there about this Psalm that stopped the mouths of Jesus' critics?

It's that they had no answers for the three great questions it posed concerning the Messiah. The first question was how David could call the Messiah 'Lord' if he was his son? We've already seen from Jesus' piercing questions that the answer to that was that Messiah had to be *more* than a man. He was to sit at Jehovah's right hand, thus placing him on an equal status with Jehovah God of Israel.

The second puzzling question they had no answer for was why David said that Messiah was to be seated in heaven at the right hand of God *before* he came to rule over his enemies. God in this passage, commands the Messiah to sit with Him in *heaven* (*not* on the earth), for an unspecified period of time *until* the Messiah would begin to rule and put down his enemies. The puzzle of this 'Great Delay' stared the Pharisees in the face and they had no answer for it.

The Pharisees agreed that a day would come when God would subject the enemies of Messiah to him by force. But how did the Messiah get to heaven, and why did he have to wait there before coming? Secondly, where did the Messiah make all his enemies, if in fact he had never been on earth before?

This Psalm leaves no other logical conclusion but that the Messiah must have lived and made enemies on earth *before* he ascended to heaven to sit at God's right hand. This 'Great Delay' in the appearance of the Messiah stands like a chasm before anyone who tries to solve the meaning of Messiah's predicted career without seeing the necessity of his having to have come twice.

## THE REASON FOR THE 'GREAT DELAY'

When Jesus was crucified, all his disciples, except John, left him, discouraged and heartbroken, partly because their dreams for the Kingdom of God on earth were now shattered. When three days later, the tomb was found empty and Jesus appeared to his followers alive, their hopes for the establishment of God's Kingdom were once again revived. Just before he left them to return bodily to heaven, he gathered them together for some last words. They asked him then if he was about to establish the promised Davidic Kingdom, smash his enemies and take over as the 'Ruling Messiah' now that he had gone through the role as 'Suffering Messiah' (Acts 1:6-11).

Jesus told them that God had fixed a time in the future when he would return to reign in that role, but, in the meantime, they were to be witnesses to the meaning of his having suffered for men's sins. Then, in plain sight of all the disciples he ascended out of sight to sit at the right hand of God until God would make his enemies his footstool. This began the 'Great Delay' in his coming in the role of conquering King.

## A 'FOREVER' PRIEST

The third great puzzling question of Psalm 110 lies in the solemn oath Jehovah God made to the Messiah in verse 4, "You are a priest forever according to the order of Melchizedek." David says here that the Messiah has been appointed as a priest forever. Now a priest is one who ministers before the Lord in behalf of the people, so obviously this means that the Messiah is ministering before God in mankind's behalf *while* he is seated at the right hand of God in the 'Great Delay,' waiting to come to earth to set up God's Kingdom.

But the question is, why would the nation of Israel need another priest, not of the regularly ordained priesthood, if the Aaronic priests were able to do their job effectively on earth? The answer is that obviously the priests must have been inadequate in some way. The priests of Israel couldn't adequately wipe out the effects of evil and sin on the part of men because they only had the impermanent system of animal sacrifices to deal with. A permanent solution was needed and Jesus, the Lamb of God, was the final sacrifice for men's sins.

## WHY THE 'GREAT DELAY?'

The last question that remains to be asked is, "Why the Great Delay in the first place?" Why didn't God just send the Messiah back immediately, bring in the promised Kingdom of peace and get on with the new world he had planned? This last answer lies waiting in another Messianic prediction, Isaiah 49:1-12. In this passage, the Messiah, called the Servant of the Lord, announces a brief survey of his future career upon the earth to the Gentiles and tells why they are even going to have the chance to learn about what he did.

The Servant first tells that God originally commissioned him to bring the nation of Israel into right relationship to God. But then he laments that all his work in that direction was an apparent failure. He says, "I have toiled in vain, I have spent my strength for nothing and vanity."

Then the Servant tells how God said to him: "It is too small a thing that you should be my servant to raise up the tribes of Jacob, to restore the preserved of Israel; I will also make you a light of the nations, that my salvation might reach to the end of the earth."

Here at last is the answer! It is too insignificant a reward for the Messiah to be the ruler over just Israel. As a reward for his sufferings, he will extend his salvation to the millions of Gentiles. But a great period of time will be needed to tell the Gentiles about Messiah and what He did for them. During this time many Gentiles and Jews will believe in him as Messiah Savior. But they must be reached during the Great Delay for at his second coming, the Messiah comes in judgment and the time for forgiveness is over.

Jesus himself as He ascended into the clouds on the Mount of Olives gave his last command to his disciples. He ordered them to go to every nation and tell what had been done for them by his death. Gentiles and Jews would then learn that there was a permanent priest at the right hand of God who would forgive them anytime during the Great Delay.

**DANIEL 9:25-26**

"So you are to know and discern that from the issuing of a decree to restore and rebuild Jerusalem until Messiah the Prince there will be seven weeks and sixty-two weeks; it will be built again, with plaza and moat, even in times of distress.

"Then after the sixty-two weeks the Messiah will be cut off and have nothing, and the people of the prince who is to come will destroy the city and the sanctuary. And its end will come with a flood; even to the end there will be war; desolations are determined."

ותדע ותשכל מן־מצא דבר להשיב ולבנות ירושלם עד־משיח נגיד שבעים שבעה ושבעים ששים ושנים תשוב ונבנתה רחוב וחרוץ ובצוק העתים:

ואחרי השבעים ששים ושנים יכרת משיח ואין לו והעיר והקדש ישחית עם נגיד הבא   וקצו בשטף ועד קץ מלחמה נחרצת שממות:

The Holocaust

## LUKE 19:41-44

And when He approached, He saw the city and wept over it, saying, "If you had known in this day, even you, the things which make for peace! But now they have been hidden from your eyes.

"For the days shall come upon you when your enemies will throw up a bank before you, and surround you, and hem you in on every side, and will level you to the ground and your children within you, and they will not leave in you one stone upon another, because you did not recognize the time of your visitation."

# The Holocaust

When Titus and the Roman legions surrounded and beseiged Jerusalem in 70 C.E., it should have come as no surprise to anyone in that city, for their great prophet Moses had clearly predicted that just such a thing would happen, and so had Jesus.

Nearly 1500 years before this devastating holocaust, Moses had warned the Jewish people that they would undergo two future judgments by God for failing to believe and follow God and His word. The first destruction of Jerusalem and dispersion of Judah's descendants took place in 586 B.C.E. by Nebuchadnezzar of Babylon. God left his chosen people in captivity for 70 years in Babylon as discipline for failing to follow his laws.

The second predicted period of discipline began with Titus' disastrous destruction of Jerusalem and the Jewish Temple in the year 70 C.E. With the slaughter of hundreds of thousands of Jews and the captivity of many more, the wandering and beleaguered nation of Israel once again was cast from her land to live as exiles and persona-non-gratis for what has amounted now to over 19 centuries.

Any person with compassion is led to ask, "Why has God dealt so harshly with his chosen people?" Tevye, in *Fiddler on the Roof*, summed it up beautifully in one of his conversations with God, when he said, "I know we're the chosen people, God. But couldn't you just choose somebody else for awhile?"

## DISCIPLINE FOR DISOBEDIENCE

The very purpose for which they were chosen has been the cause of their severe discipline from God. You see, God chose them to be a special light to the world of the truth of the one true God, Jehovah. By their love for Him and His Law and His providential care for them they were to be witnesses to an ungodly world about how to come into a right relationship with God. When they fell into spiritual darkness, as they often did, God would send along prophets to them who would harshly rebuke their sin and call them back to repentance. Sometimes they

heeded this word from God but other times they either ignored or killed the ones sent to them by God. When they did, God disciplined them more severely than the sinful pagans because His chosen people had the light of His truth and thus were without excuse for their waywardness.

That was the reason for their awesome discipline in 70 C.E. They had failed to listen to the 'Prophet' whom God had sent them, Jesus Christ, and repent of their sins and turn back to God in their hearts. Thus Moses' heartrending prediction of divine discipline fell on them:

"If you are not careful to observe all the words of this law which are written in this book, to reverence this honored and awesome name, the LORD your God, ... Then it shall come about that as the LORD delighted over you to prosper you, and multiply you, so the LORD will delight over you to make you perish and destroy you; and you shall be torn from the land where you are entering to possess it.

"Moreover, the LORD will scatter you among all peoples, from one end of the earth to the other end of the earth: ... and among those nations you shall find no rest, and there shall be no resting place for the sole of your foot; but there the LORD will give you a trembling heart, failing of eyes, and despair of soul.

"So your life shall hang in doubt before you; and you shall be in dread night and day, and shall have no assurance of your life ..." (Deuteronomy 28:58-68).

## DANIEL'S INCREDIBLE TIME TABLE

How can anyone be sure that the dispersion of the Jews from Israel in 70 C.E. and the destruction of their Temple was in accordance with what the prophets had predicted?

The main prophetic passage in the Old Testament which pinpoints this is that of the Hebrew prophet Daniel who was, himself, in dispersion in Babylon with the rest of his nation when he wrote his remarkable prophecy of Daniel 9:24-27.

In this amazing prediction of the future events of Israel's career, Daniel set forth a divinely ordained time period of "seventy weeks" of years (490 years) in which God would, in specific ways, *deal with the sin of the nation, bring in everlasting righteousness*, and *send the Messiah to the world*. This allotted time period was like a great divine "time-clock" with 490 years of time marked off on it.

A specific event was to mark the beginning of this 490 years of God's unique dealing with his people. Daniel said that when the permission was officially given for the Jews to leave their Babylonian captivity and return to their land and restore and rebuild Jerusalem, that would mark the start of this 490 year period. Like a great stop-watch, God's finger pushed down on the button and the 490 year allotted coutdown began clicking off April, 444 B.C.E.. Archaeologists have confirmed to us that that was the year that Artaxerxes Longimanus, the Persian King, gave the Jews permission to leave their exile in Babylon.

Then Daniel predicted a strange thing. He said that after sixty-nine weeks of years (483 years) had clicked off on this allotment of time, the Messiah of Israel would be revealed to the Jews and then *killed*, and the city of Jerusalem and their Temple would be destroyed and their 490 year special time allotment would be temporarily cut short by 7 years.[1]

There's no possible way that it could be coincidence that on the *very day* that Jesus rode into Jerusalem on a donkey and presented himself to Israel as their Messiah, exactly 483 years had transpired since the proclamation given by Artaxerxes. Daniel said that the city and Temple would be destroyed following the death of their Messiah and within forty years the Roman Holocaust had taken place.

There's one critical fact that must be pointed out in this prophecy. *Whoever* the Messiah was to be, he had to have come to Israel *before* the city and Temple were destroyed in 70 C.E. Only one candidate fits that role—Jesus of Nazareth!

---

[1]For fuller amplification of this prophecy see *Daniel's Prophecy of the Seventy Weeks*, Alva J. McClain, Zondervan Publishers.

## JESUS PREDICTED JERUSALEM'S DESTRUCTION

Jesus himself had thoroughly studied this prophecy of Daniel and related its meaning to his disciples. During the last week before his death, Jesus startled his disciples by telling them that the Temple was going to be destroyed.

Naturally the disciples wanted to know when this would occur. He said that the city would be destroyed shortly after he left the earth. Then he added something which Daniel hadn't predicted, but Moses had: " ... Jerusalem would be trampled under foot by the Gentiles until the times of the Gentiles were fulfilled" (Luke 21:23, 24).

The destruction of the city in 70 C.E. began the long period called by Jesus the "times of the Gentiles." As Moses predicted, during this long period the Jewish people would be wanderers from place to place with no assurance of safety or acceptance.

For nearly two thousand years now, this prophecy has been a horrible reality in the life of God's chosen people. No nation in the history of the world has undergone such persecution and distress. Even though Israel is now partially back in her ancient homeland, she isn't at peace with the world around her. Until Messiah comes again and Israel turns to him, the nation is still officially under God's divine discipline.

## NO JOY OVER DISCIPLINE

Although the nation of Israel rejected Messiah when he came 2000 years ago and the grief she's experienced since then is mainly due to that fact, that doesn't lessen the great heartache that true believers in Messiah-Jesus feel for the plight of Israel. We look on in compassion at her sufferings and pray fervently for the peace of Jerusalem.

We have one thing to give substance to our hope for Israel. We know that God will never break a promise and He still owes Israel seven years of her allotted 490 years in which to bring about righteousness in her land and purge her people of their sin. Then God's Messiah will come again to Israel and give to those of His chosen people and the world who receive Him, the Kingdom of God which He promised so long ago.

### ZECHARIAH 14:4

And in that day His feet will stand on the Mount of Olives, which is in front of Jerusalem on the east; and the Mount of Olives will be split in its middle from east to west by a very large valley, so that half of the mountain will move toward the north and the other half toward the south.

וְעָמְדוּ רַגְלָיו בַּיּוֹם-הַהוּא עַל-הַר הַזֵּיתִים אֲשֶׁר עַל פְּנֵי יְרוּשָׁלִַם מִקֶּדֶם וְנִבְקַע הַר הַזֵּיתִים מֵחֶצְיוֹ מִזְרָחָה וָיָמָּה גַּיְא גְדוֹלָה מְאֹד וּמָשׁ חֲצִי הָהָר צָפוֹנָה וְחֶצְיוֹ-נֶגְבָּה:

# The Second Coming

### MARK 14:61-62

But He kept silent, and made no answer. Again the high priest was questioning Him, and saying to Him, "Are You the Christ, the Son of the Blessed One?" And Jesus said, "I am; and you shall see the Son of Man sitting at the right hand of Power, and coming with the clouds of heaven."

# The Second Coming

From the dawn of time, man has longed for a day when the earth would put away war, when we would know equality and freedom from prejudice, when there would be abundance of food and necessities for all and when the planet would be fit for all men to live and work on in peace.

## NO PEACE WITHOUT MESSIAH

This aspiration that a day is coming when the world will finally learn to live in peace is what keeps statesmen and world leaders desperately searching for ways to make it happen. But the tragedy is that they refuse to even consider what God says in the Bible is the only way this universal peace will ever come about.

For instance, the verse engraved on the cornerstone of the United Nations' Building in New York, " ... And they will hammer their swords into plowshares, and their spears into pruning hooks. Nation will not lift up sword against nation, and never again will they learn war (Isaiah 2:4)," is taken *out of* a context in the Bible which clearly predicts that the world will never realize this peace until Messiah, the Prince of Peace, comes back to the earth to set up His Kingdom. And yet, the name of Jesus, the Prince of Peace, is not welcome in the deliberations of the nations of the world who have united in that building to try to establish world peace.

The ancient Hebrew prophets are the main source of the specific promises of a coming era of world peace and prosperity. They have not only zeroed in on its reality, but they have predicted specific details regarding when it will come, how it will be brought about, who will rule it and live in it and what life will be like in this unique time which they call the Kingdom of God.

The prophets of Israel are unanimous in saying that this Kingdom will only come about after man has gotten himself embroiled in the greatest war of all time, Armageddon, and Messiah comes to deliver those who turn to him and judge those who reject him. Those who embrace him as their savior and deliverer have a radical purification take place in their hearts which enables them to live at peace with themselves, their own families and the world.

At the same time that Messiah heals the hearts of men, he'll also restore the earth to the beauty and function he designed it for originally so that men will not only have new hearts, but a new world to enjoy it in. Isaiah says of this time that "all people who are left on earth will go up to Jerusalem to learn Messiah's ways" (Isaiah 2:3), and that "the earth will be full of the knowledge of the Lord as the waters cover the sea" (Isaiah 11:9).

Jeremiah adds this detail, "I will make a new covenant with the house of Israel after those days, declares the Lord. I will put my laws within them, and on their heart I will write them ... for they shall all know me from the least of them to the greatest ..." (Jeremiah 31:31-34). Ezekiel speaks of this same thing, "I will give you a new heart ... I will put My Spirit within you and cause you to walk in My statutes ..." (Ezekiel 36:26, 27).

Many more passages from the Hebrew prophets could be cited which show the definite teaching that only those who believe in God's Messiah and have been given this new heart, which the New Testament writers called a 'spiritual rebirth,' will enter this new world that Messiah will bring when he returns. This future world will be one of perfect environment because the One who made it will be ruling over it and only those whose hearts have been cleansed from sin and its ugly consequences will live in it.

## SIGNS OF MESSIAH'S COMING

If the Hebrew prophets are right and if Bible expositors have correctly interpreted their predictions of a coming Kingdom of God and the corresponding appearance of the Messiah, then what are some of the signs that might show us when this will occur? Are we anywhere near that momentous event?

One of the strongest emphases of Jesus'

teachings was that he would personally return back to this earth one day and that men could know when that would be by observing the signs laid out in the Scriptures by both he and the prophets. Jesus was explicit in his predictions about world conditions at the time of his return to earth. The New Testament writer, Matthew, records that the disciples of Jesus came to him privately and asked, "… what will be the sign of your coming and of the end of the age?" (Matthew 24).

## WATCH FOR THESE SIGNS

Jesus then gave them a list of signs to look for. He said that many *men would arise calling themselves Messiah*, but they would be false. Today there has been a rash of this with various gurus claiming to be the Lord from heaven.

He said *there would be wars and rumors of wars*. In other words, *hot* wars and *cold* wars. Is there anyone who would deny that this century has seen the greatest loss of human life, directly and indirectly, as the result of wars? Millions of Russians, Chinese and Europeans have been slaughtered by tyrants in just the last 50 years.

Jesus predicted *a great outbreak of worldwide famine* on a scale never before known to man. Today the headlines of Time, Newsweek and the daily newspapers scream out the devastating facts that millions are dying of starvation right at this moment. And the forecast is that millions more will starve within the immediate years ahead and there is virtually nothing being done about it, nothing, in relationship to the need!

Jesus said that *plagues would sweep the world* prior to his return. For years now, scientists have felt that the great plagues that used to threaten mankind were virtually under control. But in just the past few years great epidemics have killed millions and even though vaccines are available against some of them, there's no way to innoculate the world's masses.

*A great increase in lawlessness and inhumanity to man* would also be prevalent in the days just preceding Jesus' second coming. He also warned *that earthquakes would increase in intensity and frequency* as this old earth prepared for its final cataclysm.

## THE PUZZLE FALLS TOGETHER

The events leading up to the coming of Messiah-Jesus are strewn throughout the Old and New Testament prophets like pieces of a great jigsaw puzzle. The key piece of the puzzle which was missing until our time, was that Israel had to be back in her ancient homeland, reestablished as a nation. When this occurred in May of 1948, the whole prophetic scenario began to fall together with dizzying speed.

Since that time many crucial alignments of world powers, which were predicted would happen, began to re-shuffle and fall into their prophetic pattern. I only have space here to give the barest outline of them but extensive documentation is available for anyone wishing to pursue it.[1]

The Arabs began to unite under the leadership of Egypt in an alignment dedicated to destroying Israel. This was anticipated by Daniel and Ezekiel. The Russians have become a great world power which is aligned with the Arabs against Israel exactly as Ezekiel and Daniel said they would. In the orient a great military power has arisen which can field an army of over 200 million soldiers, the *exact* number predicted of them in the Book of Revelation.

One of the most significant prophetic signs is the emergence of a super economic and soon-to-be political power in the West in the form of the European union. The books of Daniel and Revelation predict that a confederacy of 10 nations, made up of the peoples of the ancient Roman Empire will be this power.

Zechariah, over 2500 years ago, predicted that Jerusalem would become a burden to the whole world and would set off the last great world war, Armageddon (Zechariah 12:3, 4). After the Yom Kippur war, we learned that what troubles the Arabs can trouble the whole world—oil!

But as black as this picture looks, the future was never brighter because as things get tougher in this old world, it only means that Messiah-Jesus' coming is that much nearer!

---

[1]*The Late Great Planet Earth*, Hal Lindsey, Zondervan Publishers; and *Armageddon: Oil and the Middle East Crisis*, John Walvoord, Zondervan Publishers.

# The Coming King

**PSALM 2:11, 12**

Worship the Lord with reverence, and rejoice with trembling. Do homage to the Son, lest He become angry, and you perish in the way, for His wrath may soon be kindled. How blessed are all who take refuge in Him!

עבדו את-יהוה ביראה וגילו ברעדה ׃ נשקו בר פן-יאנף ותאבדו דרך
כי-יבער כמעט אפו אשרי כל-חוסי בו ׃

**REVELATION 3:20**

Behold, I stand at the door and knock; if any one hears My voice and opens the door, I will come in to him, and will dine with him, and he with me.

# The Coming King

The first book of the Bible, Genesis, begins the story of man on earth in a paradise and the final book of the New Testament, Revelation, has man back in paradise again. But the story of what goes on in between is an epic of love and hate, good and evil, light and darkness, hope and despair and triumph and defeat. But God, who had the *first word* with mankind will also have the *last.*

Man has always been the center of God's love and concern, even after he sinned and turned in rebellion from God. In fact, that very act prompted God to put into action what might be called "Operation Promise." God promised Adam and Eve that a seed of woman would one day come and undo the damage Satan had done to mankind *and* rectify the fallout of that evil in the earth itself.

This is the story the Bible tells, from cover to cover. God's Promised One became the center of the hopes and dreams of a special race of people that He raised up from the seed of Abraham, Isaac and Jacob; the people known as the Chosen Race, the Jews. Through them, the hope of their oft promised Deliverer and His kingdom of love and peace was spread throughout the world until many people began to unconsciously hope that such a kingdom of peace would one day come.

## NO KINGDOM WITHOUT A KING

However, when a man appeared on the scene in Jerusalem 2000 years ago, claiming to be the Promised Messiah and presented his credentials of fulfilled prophecy in his life, the people who had so eagerly waited for God to send them His Anointed One, rejected him and his offer to set up the Kingdom of God right then. It must be noted here, however, that it wasn't the average man of Israel who resisted Jesus' claims of Messiahship. Thousands and thousands of Jews did believe his message and experienced a spiritual rebirth as they freely accepted Jesus' offer to forgive their sins and impart God's divine life into them.

The real resistance to Jesus and rejection of him as King must be laid squarely at the feet of the religious leaders who were the custodians of God's Word and who knew the predictions of his promised deliverance. They allowed tradition, prejudice, pride and favor to blind them to the truth of their own prophets. When they rejected their King, the Kingdom of God was postponed on earth. No King! No Kingdom!

## AN INTERLUDE OF SUFFERING

As Jesus himself predicted, when the nation didn't receive him as their Messiah, they came under the most severe discipline of God in their entire history to that point. Within forty years their city was destroyed and the Temple that had meant more to them than their Messiah, was torn down, stone by stone, and has never been rebuilt to this day. The people were slaughtered and scattered across the face of the earth. They knew nothing but heartache and opposition for the next 19 centuries.

But because their Kingdom was rejected by them, it really worked out for the good of the Gentiles because God took his 'turned down' Kingdom, and offered it to anyone, Jew and Gentile, who would accept Jesus as savior now, and coming King.

## THE END OF THE AGE

So many of the Bible prophets have referred to the closing events in God's time-table of human history as "The end of the age." This is a term that includes a number of specific events that leads up to the actual culmination of normal human history on this planet and the ushering in of a brand new world.

Bible prophets aren't the only ones who have predicted that the world as we've known it for these many centuries won't continue much longer this way. Responsible economists, statesmen, scientists and ecologists are predicting doomsday for the planet and everything on it; some even are saying that we won't make it past the year 2000.

One such scientist, Professor George Wald, Nobel winning biologist of Harvard

University said recently, "Human life is now threatened as never before, not by one but by many perils, each in itself capable of destroying us, but all interrelated, and all coming upon us together. I am one of those scientists who does not see how to bring the human race much past the year 2000."[1]

Man is approaching what God has called "The end of the age" but the final finish won't be dictated by the whims of men with their fingers on nuclear buttons. God has a precise plan of action that He's already started into motion. In the last chapter, we looked at the individual pieces of a great prophetic jigsaw puzzle which are destined to fall into place, in my opinion, in the very days in which we're living. Now I want to briefly set forth the chronological unfolding and setting into place of each of these pieces.

## AS IN THE DAYS OF NOAH

When Jesus' disciples asked him how they would know when he was about to return to them, he gave his reply in an historical allegory (Matthew 24:32-44). He said his coming would be similar to the days of Noah. People would be going about their business as usual—eating, drinking and marrying—but paying no attention to Noah's warnings about God's impending judgment. Then God put all those who believed Noah's preaching into a boat and they were delivered just before terrible judgment fell on the unbelievers. The pattern established here was that first God would give *a prophetic warning*, then His *people would be removed* and then *judgment would fall.*

What Jesus is showing with this illustration is the pattern of how events will unfold at the end of the age. People will be going around unconcerned about God and all the prophetic warning about his coming judgment of sin. Then those who have believed in him as savior, thus becoming true children of God, will be taken out of the world and great judgment will fall on those left.

This great time of tribulation will last for seven years during which God seeks, by taking away from man every other hope, to

---

[1]Midnight Magazine, October 14, 1974.

draw him to Himself. Millions will believe in the message of 144,000 Jewish evangelists who have come to see that Jesus was their Messiah. These seven years in which they seek to turn men's hearts to God are those seven years that the nation was cut short when they crucified their Messiah. They have the opportunity at that time to more than make up for failing to be God's witnesses during their history.

## DO HOMAGE TO THE SON

The part of Psalm 2 which is quoted on the beautiful picture of *The Coming King* is the solemn advice that David prophetically gives to those who will be living on the earth during the awful seven years of tribulation just prior to Messiah's return to earth to set up His Kingdom. In the rest of the Psalm, David speaks of this time when his Greater Son will come to earth and find that the "nations are in an uproar and trying to cast off all influence of God."

When the Messiah, who was the *Lamb of God* but has now become the *Lion of Judah*, comes in his glory at the end of this seven years of the earth's purification, he will "stretch forth his strong scepter from Zion and rule in the midst of his enemies. He will shatter kings in the day of his wrath and he will judge among the nations" (Psalm 110).

In the light of this terrible outpouring of God's wrath upon sinful and God rejecting men, David pleads in his Psalm, "Now therefore O kings, show discernment; take warning O Judges of the earth. Worship the Lord with reverence and rejoice with trembling. DO HOMAGE TO THE SON, lest He become angry and you perish in the way, for His wrath may soon be kindled. How blessed are all who take refuge in Him!" (Psalm 2:10-12).

In Revelation 3:20 we're introduced to Jesus in his role as King. Here he graciously holds out the promise that he will personally come into our life through the door of our will if we will but invite him. We don't need to wait until God's Kingdom comes to earth and Messiah is rightfully ruling over the new world that's promised. We can experience the peace and inner joy of his Kingdom in our hearts while we wait the coming of the King.